PAUL AND THE MACEDONIANS

David A.
deSilva

PAUL and the MACEDONIANS

The Life
and Letters
of Paul

Abingdon Press
Nashville

PAUL AND THE MACEDONIANS

This book is printed on acid-free paper.

ISBN 0-687-09078-4

01 02 03 04 05 06 07 08 09 10 — 10 9 8 7 6 5 4 3 2 1

Manufactured in the United States of America

CONTENTS

How to Use
This Resource

Welcome to *Paul and the Macedonians*, a six-session study on Paul's letters to and his relationship with the Macedonian congregations. Each of the six chapters contains common elements designed to help you use this resource successfully in a group setting or as a personal study.

"Read First Thessalonians"

First you will note throughout each chapter that there are a number of subheadings that direct you to read a portion of Paul's letters. While there may also be cross references to numerous other passages in the Bible, the passage from Thessalonians or Philippians is the key to the lesson. If this is an individual endeavor, you can read the Bible references as you encounter them. Be sure to refer back to them when you consider the study and reflection activities.

Convenient Short Blocks of Text

Second you will find that the subheadings break up text into segments that are usually about two-to-three pages long. While the information in the chapter forms a coherent whole, the ideas are "sized" so that you can not only take the long view but also spend time with distinct ideas within the whole.

Study Questions

At the end of each of these divisions within the chapter are study and discussion questions that relate to that segment of the text. Many of the questions are designed to make sure you understand the biblical text. First and Second Thessalonians and Philippians are complicated pieces of Scripture, and the apostle's arguments may sound foreign or confusing to 21st-century culture.

Other questions are more analytical and ask readers to assess meanings for the original audience. That understanding leads to another level of study helps: personal reflection on what the revealed meaning of the biblical passage means and how those learnings and faithful insights can be applied to one's life.

Closing

At the end of each chapter are some suggestions for closing that apply to both a group and an individual setting. Many times you will be asked to summarize the content and import of that chapter and the selected Scripture. In each instance, you are invited to a time of prayer.

Leading a Group

The chapters in this study are long; if you teach a group, consider taking more than one week to cover a chapter. As you lead the group, keep these pointers in mind as you plan the study session:

• Read the entire chapter, including all the Scriptures.
• Think about your group members: their needs, their experience with the Bible and with each other,

their questions. From this information, establish one or two session goals.

- Pay particular attention to the study questions and select at least one or two questions, if possible, from each segment of the text. Keeping in mind your group and your goals, note which questions you intend to cover. Try to have a variety of content, analytical, and personal application questions and activities.

- Encourage group members to use their Bibles and to read these texts.

- Be comfortable with silence and give group members a chance to think. Be sure that no one dominates and that everyone has the opportunity to participate.

- Have an intentional closure to the session by engaging in the suggested prayer or other spiritual discipline.

- Accept our best wishes and blessings for a transformational and edifying study time.

INTRODUCTION

Paul's letters to the Christians in Thessalonica and in Philippi may not feature the great theological theme of "justification by faith" (mentioned only in Philippians 3:9). However, they have much to say about how the Christian who has been forgiven by God and welcomed into God's family is to live with that family in the midst of a world that is not supportive of his or her faith.

The Macedonian Congregations

First Thessalonians addressed Christians whose neighbors looked askance at their religious commitments and sought to pressure them back into conformity with the larger culture through shaming and other challenges. Paul helped the believers interpret these experiences in light of God's perspective, reaffirmed the nobility of the believers' life in Jesus, and instructed them on sustaining one another and living so as to give no legitimate excuse for society's hatred and suspicion. Second Thessalonians continued to address these needs, adding some challenging directions regarding discipline within the church.

If Galatians was Paul's charter for Christian liberty, Philippians was Paul's charter for Christian unity. Paul addressed those who had been his partners in the faith and in mission but who had been distracted from their high calling by internal competition, posturing, and discord. He applied as a remedy the example of Jesus, the one with every claim to recognition and precedence, who instead took the form of a slave, giving us a timely prescription for cultivating a healthy culture in our congregations today.

Looking Ahead to the Future

A theme common to all three letters is the direction to look ahead to the future that God has prepared for God's people and for the world. No Christian has yet attained the full measure of Christ. As long as we individually persist in pressing forward to the goal to which God urges us, we will not make our imagined laurels the basis for rivalry with others. All Christians have received important information about the future, particularly God's judgment. This information gives believers a great advantage over unbelievers, who are not mindful of God's judgment and thus will stand in great danger on Judgment Day. Christians, therefore, need never feel inclined to conform again to the lifestyle or values of the world outside the community of faith. Rather, the call is always to invite people outside to move inside and to conform themselves to the lifestyle and values that God commends.

Together, these three letters (First and Second Thessalonians and Philippians) tell us how to shape our own attitudes so as to reflect mature discipleship. These letters tell us how to build up a strong, harmonious community of faith that is able to support all its members in the face of an unbelieving world's attempts to erode commitment.

I THE MACEDONIAN LETTERS IN CONTEXT

The Colony of Philippi

Philippi received its name from Philip II of Macedon (the father of Alexander the Great), who took possession of the settlement in 356 B.C. The Philippi that Paul knew really took on its shape following the tumultuous civil war led by Marc Antony and Octavian (who would come to be known as the Emperor Augustus) against the assassins of Julius Caesar — Brutus and Cassius. This war came to an end near Philippi in 42 B.C., and Philippi was chosen as the site for the settlement of the veterans of the victorious army. After Octavian defeated Antony near Actium in a second civil war (31 B.C.), Antony's soldiers were honorably settled there, many of them having forfeited their claims to land in Italy. The city was strategically located on the north shore of the Aegean Sea, the smaller city of Neapolis serving, in effect, as Philippi's seaport.

Acts 16:12 accurately describes Philippi as a Roman "colony," as well as "a leading city" of Macedonia (though not its capital, which was Thessalonica). We should visualize a central city with a large amount of farmland surrounding it, the latter reflecting the original land grants to the veterans. At the time of Paul's visit, the population included the privileged descendants of these veterans, who became Roman citizens; Greeks (either descended from the inhabitants of the city before it was made a Roman colony or attracted to the city by its commercial potential); and native Macedonians. The colony appears also to have had a sufficiently significant number of Jews at the time of Paul's visit to have a designated place for prayer (a *proseuche*). Josephus collected several decrees from the cities in the Eastern Mediterranean (for example, Halicarnassus and Sardis in *Antiquities* 14.10.23-24) that allowed the Jews to construct prayer houses (*proseuchai*) for their religious observances. In Halicarnassus, their prayer house was located by a river, as it was in Philippi (Acts 16:13).

The city was administered according to Roman law, for a Roman colony was an extension of Rome itself. The citizens' identification of themselves as "Romans" (Acts 16:21) was a reflection of this pride of standing. This status provided important background to Paul's use of "political" language in this letter, calling the Christians there to remember that they were, first and foremost, a colony of the kingdom of God (Philippians 3:20). Paul may have been targeting this strong sense of political identity when he urged the Christians to display unity within their group (Philippians 2:1-4), civic unity being an essential component of conducting oneself appropriately in the body politic (*politeuesthai*; the verb used in Philippians 1:27).

Excavation of Philippi has not yet yielded a clear picture of a first-century city comparable to the results of the excavation of Corinth. The extensive development of Philippi in the later Roman Empire and in the early Byzantine period makes recovery of its first-century outline difficult. Archaeologists have found a Roman bath complex, a sanctuary dedicated to Dionysus in which women played a prominent role (both in terms of the priesthood and in terms of financial support), and a large theater that dates from the Greek period. Archaeologists have also mapped out the forum (the administrative center of the colony) with its courtyard, council chamber, and temples, as well as a commercial center to the south side of the forum.

Archaeology has also revealed a strong presence of the imperial cult in Philippi. There are inscriptions mentioning priests of the deified Julius, Augustus, and Claudius; and it is likely that the temples in the forum were dedicated to the emperors and Rome. The cult of the Roman emperors was not imposed upon the people by the emperors but rather promoted locally in the eastern provinces of the Empire as a means of showing loyalty and gratitude to the family of Augustus.

The emperors were responsible for maintaining peace (a particularly valued commodity after the devastation of the civil wars), for administering justice, for organizing relief in time of famine or other hardship. In short, the emperors were considered to provide what was normally sought from the gods; therefore, showing them thanks in the form of worship was deemed entirely appropriate.

Cults of the traditional Greek pantheon (deities such as Zeus, Apollo, Dionysus, and Artemis) also existed, as well as cults imported from the East, like the Egyptian cult of Isis and Osiris or the Phrygian cult of the mother goddess Cybele. Such religious cults, all of which fell under the heading of "idolatry" as far as Paul was concerned, were important to the inhabitants of Philippi. Honoring the traditional gods secured their favor for the well-being of the whole city. Engaging in the more exotic cults made for a more personal religious experience.

The cult of Isis, for example, offered people a goddess

who would protect them individually and also extended hope for their blessedness after death. The difference between these many cults and Christianity was that the former existed alongside other cults; but the latter would admit of no divinity except the One revealed through Jesus, which would become a grave point of controversy between the Christian community and the world it left behind.

THE COLONY OF PHILIPPI

• Reflect on the civil wars that marked the transition from Roman Republic to Roman Empire (a painless, though time-consuming, way to do this is to view the 1963 film *Cleopatra*). How would the people settled at Philippi have felt toward Octavian? How might different sectors of the colony's population have regarded Rome, both favorably and unfavorably?

• What meaning did the imperial cult and the cults of the other gods have for their participants? Why might denying the validity of these cults have been dangerous? What might have been the response of Greek and Roman citizens of Philippi to people who suddenly stopped showing support for these cults?

• What are some of the principal values and beloved institutions of your culture and country? When are Christians called to live counter to some of these values? How do non-Christians respond?

The City of Thessalonica

Lying about 100 miles west of Philippi along the *Via Egnatia*, Thessalonica also enjoyed a long history before the advent of the Romans in 168 B.C. Perhaps because it was an important port city on the Aegean Sea, it was named the Roman capital of Macedonia in 146 B.C. Thessalonica was not restructured as a Roman colony, however. As a result, more of its Greek identity survived into the Roman period than was true of Philippi.

Thessalonica continued to be governed according to a Greek constitution, with a council comprised of local aristocrats and a gymnasium complex for the education of the young as well as the promotion of Greek culture, religion, and athletics. Like Philippi, Thessalonica had also supported Antony and Octavian against Brutus and Cassius in 42 B.C. The citizens especially revered Antony, although they quickly expressed their loyalty to Octavian after the defeat of Antony at Actium ten years later.

In addition to being a thriving commercial, port city, Thessalonica was a city full of idols from which to turn (see 1 Thessalonians 1:9-10). Inscriptions, carvings, and other archaeological finds bear witness to benefactor cults, including the cult of Rome and her emperors. Coins minted at the turn of the era show the deified Julius on one side and Augustus on the reverse. An older temple was rededicated to the deified Augustus and his successors. Even Roman benefactors received cultic honors. The existence of an official called an *agonothete* suggests that athletic games or contests were held in the city in honor of the emperor on a regular basis. All this added up to a strong commitment to Roman imperial ideology in this city.

One also finds evidence of the worship of the traditional Greco-Roman divinities (including the cult of Dionysus, which was prominent in this region); mystery cults like those of Isis, Osiris, and Sarapis; and the local cult of Cabiros. The local cult of Cabiros was a religious phenomenon peculiar to Macedonia and Thrace.

Cabiros was a kingly figure murdered by his brothers but who lived on in the divine realm and whose return devotees expected. He served as an official patron deity for the city, and craftspeople and merchants especially courted his favor. The details of the cult are, as with most mystery religions, exceedingly difficult to discern with certainty. We only have inscriptions, statues, and carvings as evidence rather than literary texts devoted to telling the myth or describing the worship.

THE CITY OF THESSALONICA

• In what ways was Thessalonica's history similar to that of the history of Philippi? How did residents of both cities appear to respond to the rise of Augustus and the presence of Rome as the ruling power?
• How might the gospel of Jesus Christ have resonated with the local myth of Cabiros? Why would the message of Jesus' return be regarded as a threat to civic order, whereas the myth of Cabiros' return apparently was not?
• Why might Paul have targeted these two cities (and not, say, the smaller cities of Neapolis and Amphipolis) for the planting of Christian congregations?

Paul and the Philippian Church
Read Acts 16:6-40

Paul came into Macedonia during his second missionary journey, between A.D. 50 and 52. Philippi was the first Macedonian city Paul evangelized, and its church was the first planted on European soil. Acts 16:6-10 relates the vision Paul had of the Macedonian person pleading with him to evangelize that region and the way in which the Spirit pushed Paul's team in that direction. The Acts narrative presents a rather plausible account of the founding visit.

Paul began his ministry in Philippi by seeking out support in the Jewish community as a base for his ministry, and he found that support in the household of Lydia. We should note at this juncture how important the private household was for the growth and nurture of the early church. Hospitality was crucial for providing the missionaries with a base of operations and the converts with a place to meet for worship, prayer, teaching, and mutual encouragement. The initiative taken by Lydia also reminds us of the importance of women in the Philippian church (as elsewhere in Pauline circles). Two more such women would be named as Paul's coworkers in Philippians 4:2-3.

Paul encountered trouble when his exorcism of the demon from a fortune-telling slave left her owners without their source of profit. Economics can motivate opposition to the gospel as much as religious sensibilities. Indeed, the two were often intimately linked in the ancient world, as would be the case in Ephesus where the zeal of members of the silversmiths' guild for their patron goddess, Diana, was stoked when Paul's preaching hurt their profits (see Acts 19:21-41).

The slave owners did not charge Paul so much with depriving them of their profit but with foisting upon the Philippians a way of life that was not proper for Roman citizens, and this was not a lie. Paul called Gentiles everywhere to turn "to God from idols" (1 Thessalonians 1:9), which meant abandoning traditional Greco-Roman piety and dishonoring the gods. The slave owners also played upon anti-Jewish sentiments. Jews enjoyed the status of being members of a "tolerated religion," but Roman officials were inclined to act against Jews who openly proselytized among Gentiles.

Flogged and imprisoned without a trial, Paul turned his Roman citizenship to advantage the next morning. Imagine the city officials' horror when they learned they had illegally beaten Roman citizens in the middle of a proud Roman colony! Paul left Philippi before he might have wished; but he did not leave dishonored—something that would have been important for the church he left behind.

The Philippian church enjoyed a special place in Paul's ministry. Unlike the case with other churches (the Corinthian churches, for example), Paul accepted money from the Philippian Christians in support of his ministry (Philippians 1:5; 4:10, 14-16, 18; 2 Corinthians 11:8-9). Despite their relative poverty, these Christians also contributed in an exemplary way to the collection Paul was taking up among his Gentile churches for the impoverished Christians in Jerusalem and Judea (2 Corinthians 8:1-4).

Paul would visit the Philippians on at least two more occasions before his death. First Corinthians 16:5 and 2 Corinthians 1:16 refer to another visit to the Macedonian churches, and Acts 20:1-6 speaks of Paul spending a Passover in Philippi just prior to his return to Jerusalem in A.D. 58. It is possible, though not certain, that Paul also visited the Philippian Christians after his imprisonment in Rome. There is a continuing witness to the health of the church in Philippi in Polycarp's letter to that community written in about A.D. 110. Paul's work in that city bore lasting fruit.

PAUL AND THE PHILIPPIAN CHURCH

• Using a Bible dictionary or other study help, find a map of Paul's missionary journeys. Find Philippi and Thessalonica on the map, and reconstruct Paul's three visits to this region. How would his multiple visits have been likely to affect his relationship with these churches?

• Look closely at the verses in which Paul speaks of the Philippian Christians' partnership in his ministry. What does this say about their relationship? With what ministers and missionaries has your congregation entered into such a relationship? Does this relationship go beyond material support and prayer to forming strong bonds of partnership in a common mission?

• Jewish ethics called for people to give alms, whether much or little (see Mark 12:41-44). How did the Macedonian Christians distinguish themselves in this way? When have you shown a similar commitment to showing love through contributing to the needs of others, perhaps when your own means were not abundant?

Paul and the Thessalonian Church
Read Acts 17:1-10

After leaving Philippi, Paul and Silas traveled westward along the *Via Egnatia* toward Thessalonica. Paul preached for three sabbaths in the synagogue, after which the fledgling group of believers moved their focal point to the house of Jason, a propertied convert (His ethnic background, whether Jewish or Gentile, is uncertain.), from which point the group could continue to be nurtured and to grow. First Thessalonians gives the impression of a primarily Gentile congregation (see especially 1 Thessalonians 1:9-10), but not necessarily exclusively so. Paul may well have gathered some converts from the synagogue, and his polemic in 1 Thessalonians 2:14-16 does not necessarily indicate that Jewish Christians would be absent from the congregation.

Acts 17:2 does not mean that Paul stayed in Thessalonica only three weeks but merely that he only included a mission to the synagogue for the first three weeks of his stay. Given the fact that he plied his trade while in the city to support himself (1 Thessalonians 2:9; 2 Thessalonians 3:7-9) and also received supplemental support from his friends in Philippi several times, he was no doubt active in the city for at least a few months (Philippians 4:16).

Paul's shop may have been located in an *insula*, an apartment building with living quarters on the upper floors and artisans' shops on the main floor opening onto the street. Such a location would also have afforded him access to other artisans and to those who frequented the busy center of the pre-industrial city. Artisans and manual laborers were certainly part of the church (see 1 Thessalonians 4:10b-11), along with those who were relatively well off (like Jason) and those who were poor (yet still charitable!).

The Christian group grew, thanks to the hospitality of Jason and the leadership of Paul. Paul was forced to leave prematurely (1 Thessalonians 2:17). He departed Thessalonica for points west — Beroea, Athens, and eventually Corinth (Acts 17:10; 18:17), where he would stay for almost two full years and where he would write First Thessalonians. This itinerary is fairly well reflected in 1 Thessalonians 2:17–3:6, save for one detail. According to Acts 17:14-15 (written by Luke), Timothy and Silas remained in Beroea; and Paul went to Athens alone. Timothy and Silas rejoined Paul in Corinth (Acts 18:5). In First Thessalonians, Timothy (at least) accompanied Paul to Athens and then was sent back to Thessalonica to encourage the believers and to report on their condition to Paul in Corinth. In such cases, it is usually better to rely on Paul's firsthand account of the events rather than on Luke's secondhand, and often incomplete, account.

PAUL AND THE THESSALONIAN CHURCH

• What role did hospitality play in the growth of the Philippian and Thessalonian churches? How might meeting in private houses have shaped the sense of belonging and sense of family that soon emerged as a distinctive feature of the early church? Do you know of instances where small group meetings in homes have strengthened a modern church's sense of being a family?

• Why, do you think, did Paul work to support his own ministry? Do you have more respect for full-time professional ministers or for those who engage in "tentmaking ministries"? Why?

Ancient Letter Writing and Paul's Epistles

The "letter" was a familiar device of communication in the ancient world, one that Paul adapted for his purposes. He was building, however, on well-established conventions, both in terms of the form in which a letter should be structured and what kinds of goals were appropriate for letters.

We are familiar with such conventions in our own letter writing. For example, we begin with "Dear So-and-So," even if the person is not especially "dear" to us, and tend to close with "Sincerely, Me," as though our letter needed some closing assurance of our honesty. If we were to modify this formula, the fact that there is a recognizable formula to be modified would make those changes meaningful for our reader. Thus to begin "My dear So-and-So" or "Precious So-and-So" or simply "So-and-So" all convey some added meaning because of the departure from convention.

Letters in the ancient world tended to begin with a salutation ("X to Y, Greetings"), followed by a thanksgiving or a "wish prayer" concerning the recipient, the letter body (disclosing its main purpose), and a brief closing expressing a wish for the recipient's well-being. Paul followed this basic format but expanded it at several points. Thus he began his letters with the usual "Sender to Recipient" formula but might significantly expand his self-description or the description of the recipients.

These expansions sometimes signaled matters of concern to him that would be developed at length in the letter. Moreover, Paul modified the standard "Greeting" (*chairein*) to "Grace (*charis*) and peace to you," a clever and potent reminder to the hearers that they had left behind the world of "business-as-usual" and had entered the sphere of God's favor and calling. Paul's expressions of thanksgiving and prayers on behalf of the hearers were also much richer and longer than the stereotyped, often perfunctory, expressions one finds in standard letters. These opening sections also tended to provide the recipients with a preview of topics that would be important for the letter as a whole.

Ancient letters also tended to belong to one (or more) of a limited number of types of letter, classified according to the purpose or effect the letter was meant to have. We today are familiar with a number of letter types. We write "letters of recommendation" for students or colleagues. We receive "letters of solicitation" every day, offering some product or service. We enjoy "letters of friendship" as the means by which we keep in touch with family or friends who live at a distance; and these are often also "letters of information," newsy letters keeping us abreast of developments in the lives of people important to us. Ancient teachers of the art of letter writing highlighted the following types:

• "friendly," expressive of mutual concern, partnership, and sharing of resources;
• "commendatory," recommending some person as honorable and reliable;
• "consoling," expressing sympathy toward those who have suffered unpleasant things and trying to make the hardship easier to bear;

• "admonishing," identifying inappropriate behavior and prescribing a remedy;
• "threatening," when the sender seeks to make the recipient afraid of past or future misdeeds;
• "praising," when the sender commends the recipient for past actions;
• "advisory," recommending one course of action over another;
• "supplicatory," making requests of the recipient;
• "accounting," when the sender explains why he or she has not, or will not, be able to do something expected of him or her;
• "congratulatory," expressing joy at honors or good things that have come to the recipient;
• "thankful," expressing gratitude toward the recipient for past acts of kindness;
• "apologetic," defending oneself against charges made by the recipient or a third party;
• "moral," instructing the recipient on virtuous behavior;
• "prayerful," expressing the content of prayers offered on behalf of the recipient;
• "reporting," updating the recipient on events known to the sender;
• "didactic," teaching the recipient about some topic;
• "censuring," making the recipient ashamed of some past action;
• "encouraging," making the recipient bold in pursuit of some course of action;
• "mixed," combining two or more of the above types.

Paul's letters were longer than most ancient letters and always fell into the category of the "mixed" type—the letter that sought to accomplish several goals in a single communication. Nevertheless, each smaller section of a Pauline letter could be heard as representing a single letter type. It is often a helpful guide to interpretation to think about how Paul's readers would have heard each paragraph (that is, as accomplishing the goals of a "letter of friendship" or "letter of commendation" or "letter of reproach").

ANCIENT LETTER WRITING AND PAUL'S EPISTLES

• Compare 1 Thessalonians 1:1; Philippians 1:1-2; Philemon 1-3; Galatians 1:1-5; and Romans 1:1-7. How did Paul expand the standard letter opening? The last three show significant expansions. How might these be relevant signals in letters that would go on to (a) ask for a big favor (Philemon); (b) seek to restore the apostle's authority where rival teachers had weakened commitment to Paul's gospel (Galatians); and (c) seek to secure a church's support for a missionary they had not yet met (Romans)?

• Review the list of goals letters tended to be used to achieve (the "Letter Types"). Read through one of the Macedonian letters paragraph by paragraph and ask yourself, *How would the recipients have heard this paragraph? What would they have understood Paul's goal to have been in that segment of the letter?* Is there a particular type of goal that keeps returning, that you might view as the primary type?

IN CLOSING

• What are the most meaningful insights and challenges that you have encountered in this portion of your study? How do you hope your study of the Macedonian letters will address or refine these insights and challenges?

• Pray together for openness as you study these letters and for the courage to respond in obedience to God's words to you.

II SUSTAINING FAITH IN A HOSTILE WORLD

A Dangerous Faith
Read 1 Thessalonians 1:1-10

Paul and his team were forced to flee Thessalonica before they were ready to move on. The image of being "bereft" or "made orphans" in 1 Thessalonians 2:17 confirms the impression of hasty and untimely departure we get from Acts 17:5-10. The same social forces that pressured Paul into leaving continued to apply pressure to the converts Paul left behind. Paul wrote of the "persecution" his converts endured (1 Thessalonians 1:6; 3:2-4) as well as of their suffering (2:14).

Why would the new Christians' neighbors respond with hostility to their conversion? The answer can be found in the two components of the Thessalonians' conversion recalled in 1 Thessalonians 1:9-10. In turning "from idols," the Gentile converts left behind all traditional expressions of piety, of loyalty and gratitude toward the gods and the emperor upon whose collective favor the well-being of the city depended, and of solidarity with their neighbors. To avoid all idolatry was to withdraw from most civic festivals and even social engagements, since "pagans" were scrupulous to acknowledge the gods at virtually every gathering.

In looking for the return of Jesus, the Christians were acknowledging the leadership of one who had been executed as an enemy of the state; outsiders would have viewed his return as a threat to the Roman peace. Most of the converts' neighbors would have sought their security in the belief that Rome would rule forever and thus maintain peace. Christians would look suspiciously like revolutionaries who anticipated the downfall of Rome. We should not imagine that Christians were being rounded up for the lions, however. Martyrdom was far from common in the first century, although it would become quite common in the second and third centuries.

Paul's first challenge in addressing the fledgling church (for First Thessalonians was written within a few months of Paul's departure from Thessalonica) was to insulate the believers from the pressure, censure, and hostility they faced as a result of their conversion. He needed to assure them that, despite all appearances, they were actually in a position of honor, privilege, and favor where God was concerned.

A DANGEROUS FAITH

• Reflect on the experiences of groups that have faced tension with, and even persecution from, their neighbors in America (for example, civil rights groups, abortion clinicians, replacement workers in labor strikes, representatives from both sides of the gay rights debates). Why would some Americans consider these groups to be a threat to their "way of life"? What was the goal of applying pressure? Now imagine yourself a concerned citizen of Thessalonica. Why would your neighbors' devotion to this Jesus disturb you? What might you fear from their continued existence and growth? What would motivate you to respond with hostility rather than toleration to those "Christians"?

• Today many more Christians are being persecuted globally by their neighbors for their commitment to Jesus than was the case even in the second century. Familiarize yourself with the situation of Christians in at least two countries where Christians are not tolerated (see, for example, *www.persecution.com, www.persecuted.org, or www.amnesty.org*). What do Christians living under such conditions need to hear? What can you personally do to encourage them in their contest?

God's Perspective on the Believers' Choices

First Thessalonians 1:2-3 follows the form of ancient letters by expressing a thanksgiving and mention of prayer on behalf of the recipients (although Paul's is more elaborate than the perfunctory expressions common to ancient letters). Giving thanks to God for what the Thessalonians had done and continued to do was a strategic way of informing the believers that their choices and commitments, though opposed by their neighbors, had positive value in the sight of God. Paul wrote of their investment of their resources in the Christian venture (their "work of faith and labor of love"; 1:3) and of their commitment to persevere rather than cave in to outside pressure (their "steadfastness of hope"; 1:3) as, in effect, the working out of God's desire for the group. Therefore thanks were due to God as the source of their conversion and their ongoing commitment.

God's approval of the believers continued to be an important theme as Paul elaborated on this thanksgiving in 1 Thessalonians 1:4-10. The Thessalonian converts were where they were precisely because God had "chosen" them — selected them from among their neighbors for a very special privilege. That privilege was expressed in this letter mainly as deliverance "from the wrath that is coming" (1 Thessalonians1:10; see also 3:13; 5:9, 23), that is, from the pouring out of God's judgment on a disobedient world, or as entrance into God's "kingdom and glory" (2:12). Because of the firm expectation of the Day of Judgment, the believers would value God's approval much more than they feared their neighbors' disapproval.

While the Thessalonian Christians' rejection of idols

and their commitment to Jesus might have cost them the respect and approval of their non-Christian neighbors, Paul underscored at the outset of his letter what their conversion did for their fame beyond their city (1 Thessalonians 1:7-10). The Thessalonian Christians gained a positive reputation throughout the Christian circles of Macedonia and the newly founded churches in Achaia (Corinth and Cenchreae in southern Greece). As a result, even as Paul spread the gospel, he encountered people who had already heard about the Thessalonian Christians' conversion and about their courage in the face of opposition. Paul informed the Thessalonians that they were even held up as exemplary in other Christian churches! The whole section thus took on the tone of a congratulatory letter as Paul sought to encourage the believers, showing them that any loss of local reputation was compensated for many times over in the international fame and respect they had acquired.

GOD'S PERSPECTIVE ON THE BELIEVERS' CHOICES

• Reflect on the emotional and spiritual needs of people who encounter serious opposition for their beliefs and for their commitment to an unpopular cause. Reread 1 Thessalonians 1:1-10. What needs did Paul address in this opening paragraph? What specific strategies did he use to provide the converts with affirmation and encouragement so as to enable them to persevere?

• How can you apply Paul's strategies to encourage fellow Christians locally and globally?

• Reflect on the themes of being "chosen" by God, being an "example" to other Christians, and hoping for deliverance from God's wrath. How do these concepts currently affect your perception of yourself and the decisions you make every day? How might these concepts energize your discipleship?

A Model of Integrity
Read 1 Thessalonians 2:1-12

Paul began the main body of the letter with a section that almost looks apologetic, developing a theme announced in 1 Thessalonians 1:5, namely, "what kind of persons we proved to be." That is, Paul appears to be defending himself against attacks on his character. It was indeed possible that the non-Christians would seek to erode the believers' commitment in part by trying to paint Paul as a cowardly charlatan like so many other peddlers of philosophies who had duped their converts for personal gain. In this reading, Paul sought to demonstrate his team's integrity so that the believers would continue to have confidence that their conversion experience was real and that their leaders were credible.

Paul need not, however, have composed 1 Thessalonians 2:1-12 in response to a mudslinging campaign. Part of Paul's strategy of insulating the believers against the negative opinion of non-Christians included showing how non-Christians lacked virtue and integrity, such that their opinion of what was noble and shameful should not sway the believers from their course. Reminding the believers of his team's integrity and virtue provided a positive counterpart to this. As virtuous people, Paul and his team could accurately tell the noble from the shameful, so that their opinion of the believers should have mattered more than the opinion of the unbelievers.

Paul recalled his ongoing preaching of the gospel despite the sufferings he endured at Philippi (1 Thessalonians 2:2) as proof of his courage, as well as proof of his sincerity. If he were engaged in preaching for personal gain, he would have given up this course of action long ago on account of the hardships it entailed. Paul especially highlighted his commitment to support himself as proof of his sincerity. Far from making money off the gospel, he believed so strongly in the message that he spent his own earnings to make it available (2:5, 9)! Moreover, he recalled with highly personal language the emotional bonds and nurturing relationships that he formed with the believers (2:7-8, 11-12). Rekindling warm and loving feelings among his recipients and touching their hearts in this letter was another important way in which Paul reminded them that what they had gained in the church compensated them for what they had lost in the world.

A MODEL OF INTEGRITY

• What are some self-serving motives for peddling religion? Think of some religious figures who have fallen under criticism as being "charlatans." What characteristics or acts of theirs have led to this criticism? Read 1 Thessalonians 2:1-12. What evidence did Paul bring forward in support of his integrity?

• Place yourself again in the Thessalonian church. Why does Paul think it is important for your commitment to the faith to be reminded of his team's integrity? How does this need intensify if outsiders are slandering Paul in your hearing?

• How have close relationships with reliable, Christian friends helped strengthen your faith or enabled you to persevere in the face of opposition? When have lapses in another's integrity made it more difficult for you to persevere in fidelity to the gospel? How do your reflections on these questions sharpen your sense of vocation in your own relationships with other people and in your own pursuit of Christian integrity?

A Model to Imitate

As people of integrity, Paul and his team were also models of the kind of behavior that God approves. For this reason, becoming "imitators" of Paul was a frequent theme in his letters (1 Thessalonians 1:6; 2 Thessalonians 3:7-9; 1 Corinthians 4:16; 11:1; Philippians 3:17).

Paul prominently professed seeking in all his actions to please God rather than desiring the approval of mortals (1 Thessalonians 2:4, 6). For many people, peddling philosophy was a means by which to increase one's reputation, one's positive fame or honor. It is only by being free from such concern for human reputation, however, that a person can be either a true philosopher or a true Christian—especially when naming Jesus as Lord brings one into disrepute with most human beings. Paul was especially zealous to have his converts follow his example in this regard, calling their attention already to the One who looked on their hearts and actions (1:3) and whose approval counted for all eternity. The focus on the Day of Judgment, when God brings all things to remembrance for praise or for censure, especially reinforced this point. Paul's team also had the courage to bear witness to the truth of God in the face of a hostile society (2:1-2), a courage that the believers also displayed in their conversion (1:6-7). This courage derived from an adequate appreciation of the importance of God's approval over human approval.

Paul also underscored his gentleness, his commitment to nurturing the community of faith (The images of nurse and father are important here.), his giving of himself for the building up of others in the church (1 Thessalonians 2:7-8, 11-12). Paul hoped his converts would all embody this quality toward one another, pouring themselves sacrificially into their "labor of love" for one another (1:3) so as to keep each one running forward toward the goal (see 3:12; 4:9-10; 5:11, 14-15).

Paul laid heavy emphasis on his working with his own

hands to support himself and his team during their ministry (1 Thessalonians 2:9) as proof of his sincerity. He also urged believers to continue to work to support themselves so that they might have means of relieving those in need (4:11-12; 5:14-15; see also 2 Thessalonians 3:7-13).

Finally, Paul presented himself as an example of not allowing temporal desires (like the desire for money, fame, or influence over others) to distract one from the one important ambition of being found "worthy of God" and being granted entrance into God's kingdom. This example intersected with the Thessalonian converts at the point of reputation (since care for reputation would tend to lead them away from the group) and at the point of sexual purity (1 Thessalonians 4:1-8). Nevertheless, greed and desire for power in the church also remained potent threats to completing the Christian race well in other first-century churches (see Philippians 2:1-4; 4:2-3; 1 Timothy 6:9-10; Titus 1:11).

A MODEL TO IMITATE

• Think about several people who have been very important in your life, especially in your faith journey. What did you learn from the example of these people? What has remained with you longer, their example or their words? Why is teaching by example so important?

• Reread 1 Thessalonians 2:1-12. What values and attitudes did Paul hope could be learned from his example? Where else in First Thessalonians are these lessons impressed upon the recipients?

• Reflect upon your own example, and ask several people what they will remember and observe about you. Are these things conducive to stimulating faith and discipleship in others? What aspects of your example might hinder rather than help advance the gospel?

Rethinking What Is "Normal"
Read 1 Thessalonians 2:13-16

"Imitation," or falling in line with a pattern, again emerges as an important theme, particularly the pattern of faithful response to God being met with persecution by a godless world. This theme was introduced in 1 Thessalonians 1:6, where the Thessalonian believers are said to have fallen in line with the pattern not only of Paul but also of Jesus himself. In 1 Thessalonians 2:14-16, that pattern is extended to include the communities of faith in Judea.

This pattern of the world's hostile response to the followers of Christ established a new definition of "normal." Jesus' obedience to God—his pursuit of the path that God approved and honored—brought him into open confrontation with and degradation at the hands of his society. The same fate, Paul averred, befell the Jewish Christian community in Judea at the hands of non-Christian Jews. The same fate befell Paul at nearly every turn as he preached the coming kingdom of the crucified King. Paul helped his converts see that what had befallen them since his departure from the city was not something unexpected or abnormal, not something that should cause them to question the choices they had made. Rather, suffering persecution is precisely the "norm" for those who do what is virtuous and right in God's sight and who seek God's approval for eternity rather than the approbation of an impious world.

Paul uncharacteristically sprayed venom toward his fellow (though non-Christian) Jews in 1 Thessalonians 2:15-16. Embarrassed by Paul's words, some scholars seek to remove the problem by calling these verses an early

Christian addition to the letter. It is admittedly a far cry from Paul's more sympathetic words in Romans 9:1-5, which was written six or seven years later.

Here, however, these harsh words served an important purpose: They reminded the audience that those who opposed the progress of the gospel were the ones who displeased God and who called down on themselves God's judgment. Their hostile Gentile neighbors were hurting themselves more than the converts by their opposition since, like the Jews who harassed the churches in Judea, they would find themselves encountering God as Judge and Avenger (see also 1 Thessalonians 5:1-3). Far from giving in to the pressure of outsiders, the converts were led to view their neighbors' hostility as a sad sign of their neighbors' own dishonor in God's sight and as a harbinger of their neighbors' own destruction.

RETHINKING WHAT IS "NORMAL"

• Read 1 Thessalonians 1:6 and 2:13-16. Trace the instances in the text in which Paul urges imitation. What value would this urging have for the persecuted converts? Why would being reminded that this was "normal" help them endure the still unpleasant opposition?

• Many people face difficult situations, temptations, or losses as if no one else has faced the same thing. They often gain strength and hope upon learning that they are not alone. When has this been your experience? Why does learning that your situation is "normal" or at least "shared" help?

• Paul was not afraid to lay out what God approves of and disapproves of, whom God will reward and whom God will condemn. How can we learn from Paul in this regard? What are the dangers of imitating Paul in this regard? For example, how have people used this kind of talk to promote cultlike forms of Christianity that deny salvation to all outside their little group or to manipulate others into going along with one's agenda? How do you hold together the fact that only God can discern the heart and the call to discern between right and wrong so that one can pursue the good?

Making Sense of Opposition
Read 1 Thessalonians 2:17–3:13

Paul revealed in this section his chief pastoral concern, that "no one would be shaken by these persecutions" (1 Thessalonians 3:3). This was a cause of anxiety to him after he was forced to leave Thessalonica (2:18; 3:5), such that he sent back his junior colleague Timothy to "strengthen and encourage" the believers (3:1-2). Paul hoped to return to continue shoring up the Thessalonian Christians' commitment to Christ and to one another and the work of insulating them against the pressures of non-Christians (3:10-11).

He sent this letter primarily to serve those very goals in the interim. Timothy had already returned to Paul with good news about the converts' commitment, with the result that First Thessalonians was not a letter of desperation (as if the converts were near to giving in to the temptation to revert to their old way of life). It was instead a letter of encouragement to them to continue fighting the good fight. We should also see Timothy's visit as Paul's opportunity to learn about specific questions troubling the community (such as would be addressed in 4:13-18) as well as other specific information about the church.

Paul continued to emphasize the predictability and normalcy of the negative response of society (1 Thessalonians 3:4), so that it would not take the believers off guard or cause them to doubt the rightness or wisdom of their conversion. He introduced, however, yet another perspective on society's hostility by placing it in the context of the cosmic battle between Satan and the angels of God. The tempter (Satan) stood behind the opposition to the believers. This opposition was a tool by which Satan attempted to defeat those who would respond to God's call and thus diminish the kingdom of God (3:5). Satan had even thwarted Paul's attempts to visit and encourage the converts (2:18), since Paul's return would increase the likelihood of Satan's purposes being defeated. The believers were thus oriented toward their neighbors' attempts at "correction" to see in them, not a legitimate critique of their new way of life, but an attack of the evil one, God's cosmic enemy. Their commitment to resist the "temptation" to yield to that pressure would be measurably strengthened as they saw behind it, not just human beings, but the devourer of souls.

MAKING SENSE OF OPPOSITION

• This section might sound to the hearers like a "letter of accounting," explaining why Paul did not come back to check on his friends and how they could know he had not abandoned them. Why would Paul feel the need to include this information? How effective is 1 Thessalonians 2:17–3:11 in providing that twofold explanation?

• Look up New Testament references to Satan or the devil. How was this figure viewed across the spectrum of early Christian writings? What were his characteristic functions? How would associating Satan with the society's pressuring the believers to revert to their old way of life affect the believers' responses to that pressure?

• Reread 1 Thessalonians 3:4-5. Paul gave the impression that persecution was part of the "cost of discipleship" and that the believers knew this when they decided still to invest themselves in partnership with Christ. Why would they have been willing to pay that price? How would remembering their earlier evaluations of the value of being associated with Christ help them now to keep braving society's rejection?

Incentives to Persevere
Re-read 1 Thessalonians 2:17–3:13

Paul's heartfelt concern for the believers, a topic of 1 Thessalonians 2:1-12, continued to come to expression in this section as well. Timothy's report also gave evidence that the converts remembered Paul and his team with love, warm affection, and deep commitment to the relationship (3:7). Paul shared that he, too, still suffered distress and persecution but that the Thessalonian Christians' steadfast commitment gave him joy and strength in the midst of his trials (2:19-20; 3:7-9). Having heard Paul express the importance of their commitment, the converts would be moved to endure, in part, so as to continue to gladden the heart of the apostle who had meant so much to them. As a result, his labors and his suffering would not be "in vain" (3:5).

A second motivation for perseverance was the eschatological horizon of which Paul refused to allow the converts to lose sight. History is rushing forward to the day of the "coming of our Lord Jesus" (1 Thessalonians 3:13). Paul looked ahead to this day as the day on which his team's obedience and achievement would be manifested and rewarded (2:19-20), and he called his converts to keep an eye fixed on that day so that they would so live in the present as to be found "blameless" (3:13). Steadfast endurance in the way of life taught by Paul, though it entails hardship in the present, remains the path to eternal safety and honor when God comes to judge.

A final resource for perseverance was the community itself—here the mutual love of believers manifested in mutual encouragement and in acts of kindness. Paul returned to this important resource throughout the letter (1 Thessalonians 3:12; 4:9-10, 18; 5:11-15). The building up of strong, close, personal, and meaningful relationships within the community of disciples was an important counterbalance to the loss of personal connections each believer had suffered on account of leaving behind his or her former way of life. In order for each individual convert to persevere, Christians must supply for one another the sense of belonging, of affirmation, and of being loved and valued that their non-Christian neighbors had taken from the converts.

INCENTIVES TO PERSEVERE

• Read 1 Thessalonians 2:1-12 and 2:17–3:13 again, carefully noting how Paul spoke about his feelings and longings toward the believers and theirs toward him. What were the signs that these parties truly valued one another and their friendship? How did stoking the fires of this friendship serve Paul's pastoral goal of strengthening the believers' commitment to their new faith? When have Christian friendships been important in your own faith journey? When have reliable, loving friends enabled you to take risks to grow in discipleship, in knowledge of God, and in Christian service?

• First Thessalonians is an excellent reflection of the apocalyptic nature of Paul's gospel, looking always ahead to God's intervention in the world and to the manifestation of God's justice that will accompany the second coming of Christ. Read 2 Corinthians 5:9-10; 2 Thessalonians 1:6-10; Hebrews 10:36-39; Revelation 1:7; 20:11-15. How important was it, in early Christian culture, to be prepared for Christ's coming? What were the consequences of being unprepared, or being found "on the wrong side"?

• Paul introduced these topics to help Christians decide each new day that Christ's friendship was worth the cost of receiving the world's enmity. How did the expectation of Christ's coming and God's judgment advance that goal? When has contemplation of the "yet to come" assisted you to live out a life of obedience and service to Christ and to avoid being unfaithful?

IN CLOSING

• Review what the first half of First Thessalonians contributes to the three goals we have identified: (1) insulating the believers against doubts or second thoughts about the wisdom of their conversion; (2) strengthening the believers' commitment to the way of life they had embraced; and (3) creating a positive model of discipleship.

• Pray for believers who seek to be loyal to Jesus and to one another in the face of a hostile society, for growth in being wholeheartedly committed to seeking God's approval rather than human esteem, and for Christians close to you whom you know to be in need of God's strengthening.

III As We Await Christ's Coming

Sexual Boundaries
Read 1 Thessalonians 4:1-8

Paul called the converts to dedicate themselves to conducting themselves according to the apostle's instructions, reaffirming for them that this was the way "to please God" (1 Thessalonians 4:1). The alternative to pleasing God was, of course, encountering God as "avenger" of wrongdoing (4:6). Again, the horizon of God's judgment — of being approved or censured by God — provided the backdrop for Christian ethics.

God's will for the believers was their "sanctification" (1 Thessalonians 4:3), a word that took on rich meanings in a world in which purity and pollution were vital concepts. Being "sanctified" meant being moved from an ordinary state to a holy state in which one could meet directly with and be in service to the divine. Both Jews and Gentiles would understand this concept well. Rituals like baptism were part of this process, and indeed the death of Jesus would later be interpreted in terms of a ritual sacrifice of consecration on behalf of believers (Hebrews 9:1–10:18). In the early church becoming "holy to the Lord" was not merely a matter of ritual but also a matter of character and behavior. To be sanctified, one had to abstain from the defilements that God abhorred and that were interpreted entirely in ethical terms in the New Testament (see Mark 7:14-23).

To be sanctified, however, is also to be set apart from the ordinary. Paul used holiness language to reinforce the social boundaries of the church. As Christians pursue holiness, they leave behind the ordinary state that continues to characterize non-Christians. Paul focused this discussion on the sexual conduct that is to characterize the Christian group and notably distinguish it from the non-Christian population. As a Christian abstains from extramarital sexual conduct and also refuses to exploit his or her marriage partner as a means of getting sexual gratification (1 Thessalonians 4:4, 6), he or she moves forward toward sanctification.

Paul was also characterizing the outside world as given over to the dishonorable state of being slaves to their passions (1 Thessalonians 4:5), which was actually a frequent theme of popular Greek and Roman ethics. In this way, sexual mores furnish another line to draw between the sanctified and the outsiders. The clearer the inside/outside boundary is drawn and the more dishonorable or disadvantageous being on the outside is seen to be, the more likely will be the believers' perseverance in the church.

SEXUAL BOUNDARIES

• Read several texts about holiness in the Bible (for example, Leviticus 11:44-45; 19:2; 20:22-26; 22:31-33; 1 Corinthians 3:17; 2 Corinthians 6:14–7:1; Hebrews 10:10-22). Why is "holiness" a positive value? What benefits or privileges does it bring? What is the significance of "holiness" for one's relationship with God? Now read 1 Thessalonians 4:1-8. How did Paul use "holiness" (sanctification) language? How does your survey of other texts enrich and inform your reading of 1 Thessalonians 4:1-8?

• What negative consequences did Paul believe to attend unbridled sexual indulgence, both within a marriage and in extramarital affairs? How might this kind of behavior be especially erosive within the Christian community? What positive consequences would attend accepting his instructions as indeed given on God's authority (1 Thessalonians 4:8)?
• Journal privately about how fully you have manifested "sanctification" with regard to sexuality. Where are you succeeding and falling short even now?

Loving God's Family
Read 1 Thessalonians 4:9-12

With this section, Paul began to respond to topics brought up by the converts and sent back to Paul via Timothy. What does it mean for us to show "sibling love" in the church? What about believers who have passed away? Have they missed their reward? What about the timing of Jesus' return? The "now concerning" (1 Thessalonians 4:9; 5:1) was also used throughout First Corinthians (see 7:1; 8:1; 12:1; 16:1) to show that Paul was not bringing up these topics on his own but in response to the believers' questions.

Paul affirmed the Thessalonian Christians in their practice of brotherly and sisterly love. Paul used the Greek word *philadelphia* here to encapsulate the attitude and ethos that were (and are) to guide Christians in their interactions with one another. The early Christians were taught to regard themselves as born anew from God, with the result that they became sisters and brothers one of another (see Matthew 12:46-50; 23:8-9; Hebrews 2:10-11; 13:1). Indeed, some biblical writers went so far as to say that the believer has left his natural inheritance behind in exchange for a new and more glorious one, which includes a new family (see 1 Peter 1:3-4, 14-19).

A well-developed ethic for kin (especially siblings) existed in the ancient world. Siblings were supposed to cooperate, not compete, with one another. "Sibling rivalry" would have been regarded as an ugly thing. Siblings were supposed to be absolutely trustworthy and reliable in their support of one another. Harmony and unity were to be the watchwords of their relationships (Philippians 1:27–2:4; 1 Peter 3:8), and these values were to be lived out in shared ideals and in the sharing of possessions (see Acts 4:32; 1 John 3:16-18). Siblings were to hide one another's shame (James 4:11; 5:9) and seek to promote one another's honor (Romans 12:10). They were also to practice reconciliation, forgiveness, and patience toward one another (Matthew 18:15-17, 23-35; Colossians 3:13-14).

Paul was content that the Thessalonians understood and demonstrated this love toward one another both in and beyond their own congregation (1 Thessalonians 4:9-10; see also 1:3). The fact that the Macedonian churches distinguished themselves in the collection for the sisters and brothers in Judea despite their own lack of abundance continued to testify to how deeply committed they were to fellow Christians as family (2 Corinthians 8:1-5).

The second emphasis in this paragraph sought to cultivate the presentation of a good face toward outsiders. While the believers were to be free from manipulation by unbelievers, Paul nevertheless urged them to live above the outsiders' suspicions of them. Paul drew on philosophical traditions here, since Plato also commended the person who lived quietly, minded his or her own affairs, and avoided being a meddler. In urging believers to continue to work at their occupations, Paul sought to distinguish Christians from Cynics. Unlike the Cynic, the Christian was not to become a parasite but rather to continue to contribute in meaningful and tangible ways to the life and welfare of society. Paul viewed labor as a noble way of life, since it provided freedom. He worked with his hands so as to be free to preach the gospel and to live beyond the constraints of having to please patrons.

LOVING GOD'S FAMILY

• Read 1 Thessalonians 4:9-12 and reflect on each of the aspects of how siblings are to manifest sibling love. Imagine how such love would have manifested itself among—and reached out beyond—the Thessalonian Christians. What would such an ethos contribute to the health and longevity of the Christian group?

• Where have you seen members of your congregation embodying "sibling love"? Where have you seen this ethos violated? What were the results? How can you take steps toward reconciliation, toward being more of a sister or brother to others in your congregation, to Christians in other folds, and to your Christian family beyond your location?

• Paul instructed his converts to embody some of the behaviors their neighbors would value, but he also drew the line at some critical points (such as idolatry, self-indulgence, and the like). Why, then, do you think he was so careful to isolate precisely the points at which Christian culture was to rub against Greco-Roman culture? Discuss the interaction between Christian culture and Western (or American) culture. Where does Christ command us to live differently? How do we, at the same time, "behave properly toward outsiders"?

Death Is Not Beyond Jesus' Reach
Read 1 Thessalonians 4:13-18

Timothy returned to Paul, bringing news of the deaths of some of the believers in Thessalonica and with a concern these deaths caused. Would these people lose out because they would not be able to meet Christ at his coming? Had they suffered the rejection of their peers in vain? Would they not enjoy the benefits for hope of which they left behind their old way of life? Fundamentally, their questions concerned which power has the final word, the gospel or death.

Jesus himself had spoken about the elect being gathered at the coming of the Son of Man (Mark 13:24-27); but, although he believed in the resurrection of the dead, he did not make this an explicit feature of his end-time scenario. Paul, however, did. He saw in the resurrection of Jesus from the dead the first fruits of a great crop to be reaped from the realm of the dead (1 Thessalonians 4:14).

Paul offered this explanation to enable the believers to grieve as people who had hope. The precise formulation of 1 Thessalonians 4:13 actually pointed out a weakness in the Greco-Roman society's understanding of reality. These people were without hope in the face of death, even with their devotion to the gods and their ideology of Roman rule. The Christians, however, had been given yet another mark that distinguished them from the unbelievers. The Christians had been entrusted with information about an eternal future with God that allowed them to put their loss of loved ones in perspective. They were by no means forbidden to grieve, but they were hereby equipped to grieve well and to trust in God's power over death.

DEATH IS NOT BEYOND JESUS' REACH

• If believers who had passed away before Christ's return missed out on their hoped-for reward at the coming of Christ (being no longer alive to meet him at his coming), what would the effect be on the harassed

Christians in Thessalonica? How would knowing that Jesus would also deliver and reward those who died in hope embolden the believers to persevere? to grieve with hope? How real is this hope to you?

The Christian's Incomparable Advantage
Read 1 Thessalonians 5:1-11

Granted, then, that God will reward the saints who are alive at Christ's coming and those who have died before Christ's coming. When will Christ's coming occur? Since the Second Coming, the day of the Lord, was such an important cornerstone of Paul's gospel and the converts' new faith, it would be quite natural for them to inquire about the proximity of this event.

Paul replied to this concern as he did in 1 Thessalonians 4:9, affirming that they already had received the information they needed to have a grasp of that topic. Rather than attempting to lay out timetables or to provide a series of signs preceding Christ's coming—a reserve that modern Christians would do well to imitate—Paul simply highlighted the suddenness of the day of the Lord. He used two images to bring this suddenness home. The first image derived from a warning of Jesus, urging the disciples to remain watchful so that they would be prepared, unlike the householder who did not know when the thief was coming (Matthew 24:42-44). The image of the Lord coming "as a thief" became quite popular in the early church (1 Thessalonians 5:2; 2 Peter 3:10; Revelation 16:15). The second image derived from Isaiah's oracle concerning the day of the Lord in Isaiah 13:6-9, likening the arrival of that day to the onset of a pregnant woman's labor pains (1 Thessalonians 5:3).

Knowing that the day was coming, and coming suddenly, however, gave the believers an enormous advantage over those outside the church. Those outside were indeed saying "peace and security" (1 Thessalonians 5:3), as Paul wrote, for these two words were key slogans of Roman imperial rule. The *pax Romana*, or "Roman peace," was the chief accomplishment of the emperors; and this "peace" was celebrated with altars, statues of the goddess *Pax*, and inscriptions on coins. Another common Roman coin reverse depicted "security" (*securitas*) personified as a woman—presented as one of the benefits the emperors conferred. Paul's gospel was indeed revolutionary in that he and his converts looked forward to the overturning of this state of affairs at the "day of the Lord" (1 Thessalonians 5:2).

Although attaching themselves to Jesus had brought the converts into conflict with their neighbors and had led to hardship, the real disadvantage, Paul said, lay with being at peace with that deluded society. In light of the coming crisis, the non-Christians were like drunken people groping about in the darkness at night, who finally fall asleep in a stupor and are completely overtaken by the calamity. Their neighbors' opposition to the believers, then, could also be understood as a symptom of their ignorance and folly. The result was that Paul's word about preparedness or lack of preparedness for the day of the Lord became another resource to help the believers persevere in their commitment to Christ and resist the pressure on them to revert.

Paul highlighted the contrasts and incompatibility between the Christians and non-Christians and thus made the boundary lines clearer and stronger (not to keep new converts out, but rather to make apostasy less appealing).

He wrote that Christians are "children of light" as opposed to children "of darkness" (1 Thessalonians 5:5). Believers belong to the "day" rather than to the "night." By emphasizing the differences in such stark ways, Paul made it more difficult for the converts to return to their old way of life.

THE CHRISTIAN'S INCOMPARABLE ADVANTAGE

• From the perspective of the citizens of Macedonia, Rome could be seen to provide a stable and secure life for her subjects. How would such people regard the growing Christian movement with its anticipation of "the day of the Lord"?

• Read 1 Thessalonians 5:1-11. How did Paul use the suddenness of Christ's return to show up the disadvantage and danger facing those who did not believe the gospel? How did this topic make the believers more secure in their decision to follow Jesus?

• The return of Christ, the "day of the Lord," pervaded Paul's thought and the beliefs and ethics of the early Christians. To what extent and in what ways does this topic support your faith and direct your life choices? How would recapturing the vividness of this expectation affect your walk of discipleship?

Living in the Light of the Day

Once again Paul shows that the privilege of knowing the truth of God comes with the responsibility of living in line with that truth. "Faith" without "deeds" was as dead for Paul as it was for James (James 2:14-26). Being a child of the day means that one must live in a manner befitting daylight, and especially in a manner befitting the day of the Lord (see Romans 13:11-14). "Sleeping" is an apt image for keeping from one's consciousness the coming visitation of God in judgment. "Drunkenness" is a similarly apt image for dulling one's spiritual alertness through indulging the passions of the flesh; losing one's focus on the eternal race through temporal distractions; and having one's perception distorted through drinking in the values and ideology of the dominant, unbelieving culture. Becoming "intoxicated" with the pursuit of money, reputation, or advancement; with the ethos of materialism and consumerism; or with the gratification of one's pride (for example, in family or church fights), appetites, or lusts is easy.

The Christian is to abstain from all such intoxicants, so that he or she may be undistracted and unimpeded from preparing for the coming of the Lord and unembarrassed about his or her past behavior when that day arrives. Instead, the Christian is to remain awake and to be sober (1 Thessalonians 5:6). The Greek verbs Paul chose (*gr_gorein* and *n_phein*) were alive with ethical resonance in early Christian and Greco-Roman culture. The first verb ("stay awake") also means "be vigilant" or "be on the lookout" and appears frequently in Jesus' instructions on the end time (see Mark 13:34-37; also 1 Peter 5:8; Revelation 3:2-3; 16:15). The second verb ("be sober") is often used, in an extended sense, to mean "exercise self-control" as well as "keep sharp."

The need for vigilance and self-control is enhanced by Paul's introduction of military imagery into the passage with the inventory of armor (1 Thessalonians 5:8). This image is based on the armor God is said to put on in preparation for the day of vengeance (Isaiah 59:17). The notion that Christians are also involved in a conflict against Satan and his minions no doubt recommends the idea that Christians, too, need spiritual armor (see the fuller development in Ephesians 6:13-17).

The image of warfare strategically influenced the way

the believers would think about the opposition they faced, propelling them forward to seek victory beyond that opposition rather than to succumb to it. In this battle, they needed to be watchful against the many ways in which the enemy (Satan) might try to weaken their defenses or to overwhelm individual believers. In their situation, keeping faith (which should be thought of here as double-sided — trust in God but also faithfulness toward God) was essential; but so was showing love within the Christian community. Love would ensure that no individual would be overwhelmed by the opposition and would supply whatever aid was lacking. Hope of deliverance — keeping their mind's eye fixed on the day of the Lord and being rescued from God's wrath by the Messiah with whom they had kept faith — was, of course, the primary defense.

Paul rounded out the discussion of the day of the Lord by returning to the use of "awake or asleep" in the sense of "alive or dead," returning thus to the theme of 1 Thessalonians 4:13-18. Paul concluded by urging the Christians to help keep their fellow believers on track and pressing forward (1 Thessalonians 5:11). A supportive and encouraging community is essential to individual perseverance in discipleship.

LIVING IN THE LIGHT OF THE DAY

• Reflect on the images of "sleep" and "drunkenness" in 1 Thessalonians 5:1-10. You may also want to ponder the "nocturnal behaviors" censured in Romans 13:11-14. How did Paul use these images and their opposites to shape the believers' ethic and to motivate them to continue to live in a manner distinct from their surrounding culture, despite the opposition that entailed?

• What are some of the worldly "intoxicants" that have a foothold in your life? From which have you learned to abstain, and how has this increased your spiritual sobriety? With regard to the day of the Lord, are you more asleep or watchful? What would need to disappear from, change in, or emerge in your life for you to be prepared for that day and not be surprised? How can you use that component of the mystery of faith ("Christ will come again.") to sharpen and deepen your walk of discipleship?

• Paul continually urged believers to look after other believers. When has the community of disciples been of such help in your journey? How have you sought to provide encouragement and assistance to fellow believers? What practical things can you and your congregation do to grow in this essential part of "being the church," with regard to fellow believers locally and globally?

Precepts for the Christian Life
Read 1 Thessalonians 5:12-22

The final section of First Thessalonians may seem like a string of unrelated instructions and precepts, especially the staccato commands of 5:16-22. This impression is not entirely incorrect, although there is a little more logic and organization to Paul's list than meets the eye at first.

The first set of instructions addresses how believers are to treat those who have the responsibility of leading the congregation (1 Thessalonians 5:12-13; see also Hebrews 13:17). Paul did not speak of a professional clergy class but rather of "lay leaders" of the congregation. These people were the patrons of the community, the believers who had both the time and the resources to devote themselves to building up the community. It is noteworthy that Paul highlighted their labor and service as the ground for their esteem, not their wealth or position. This was not only a word to the congregation, who were instructed to show gratitude for the leaders' generous investment of themselves in the community. It was also a word to the patrons, who were to recognize that their calling was to serve and strengthen the whole community rather than to lord it over their fellow believers. If both parties adopted these attitudes, then the congregation would indeed enjoy "peace" (1 Thessalonians 5:13) rather than tensions and factionalism.

The second set of instructions addresses the responsibility of every believer toward other believers (1 Thessalonians 5:14-15). The "idlers" (*ataktoi*) will become a prominent concern in 2 Thessalonians 3:6-15 and will be studied more closely below. With regard to the other groups, we find Paul again reminding the Thessalonian Christians of their responsibility toward those sisters and brothers who were having difficulty remaining committed to the walk of discipleship (either on account of opposition from outside or on account of the intrinsic challenges of following Jesus). For believers facing hard obstacles, a word of encouragement or a show of support at a critical moment can make the difference between persevering and giving up.

Finally, Paul expressed in his own words a principle well attested in the Jesus tradition (see Matthew 5:38-48; Luke 6:27-36): Rather than react with evil intent toward another's evil intent, let God's generosity and goodness guide your every deed (1 Thessalonians 5:14-15). Even in a situation of persecution, Paul refused to allow his converts to fail to apply this principle to either their non-Christian neighbors or to other believers (5:15). By showing a generous heart, the believer might quite possibly defuse a non-believer's suspicion and hostility.

The third set of instructions (1 Thessalonians 5:16-18) calls for the Christian to make joy, prayer, and thanksgiving to God the hallmarks of every hour and of every situation (see also Philippians 4:4-7). "Rejoice" (joy) does not mean acting as if everything is "enjoyable," for much of life is quite painful; but it does mean holding on so firmly to God's goodness and promises that these become a centering place of joy in the midst of all circumstances. Similarly, "giving thanks" in the midst of every circumstance does not mean feigning thankfulness for every circumstance. It does, however, call for mindfulness of God's gifts and watchfulness for how God will work in and through those circumstances for the growth and benefit of God's children. In the midst of life, it is fitting also to be in constant conversation with God. We are to seek God's guidance so as to be useful to God's purposes and God's church at every turn. We are to bring the needs of the church and the world ever before God (including the missionaries, 1 Thessalonians 5:25; see also 2 Corinthians 1:10-11), and, in short, attune our hearts to God's heart in all times and places.

The final set of instructions (1 Thessalonians 5:19-22) encourages believers to allow the Spirit to move through and use them in corporate worship. Paul emphasized the gift of prophecy (not foretelling events so much as bringing a relevant word of guidance or direction from God), which he also preferred in 1 Corinthians 14. At the same time, Paul sought to regulate those gifts, encouraging the congregation to examine the manifestations against known standards (like Scripture, Paul's instruction, and the inward testimony of the whole congregation) so as to discern between what came from God and what came from the enemy (Satan).

PRECEPTS FOR THE CHRISTIAN LIFE

• Read 1 Thessalonians 5:12-15 and reflect on each instruction. If the audience heeded Paul's words, what kind of community would they be? How effective would such a church be in terms of membership retention, individual growth, and outreach? Where is your faith community strong in terms of modeling such an ideal? Where does it need to grow, and how can you help it do so?

• What is Christian "joy"? Have you encountered models of Christian "joy" that you considered superficial and others that seemed deeply rooted? What made the difference? How would Christian joy, gratitude, and prayer provide a stabilizing center for the soul? How strong is this center in your life?

• Read 1 Corinthians 12 and 14 as background to the kind of experience Paul referred to more briefly in 1 Thessalonians 5:19-22. How did Paul envision the Spirit working in the congregation, both in its worship life and beyond? What would be the disadvantages of "quenching" the Spirit? What dangers might attend the uncritical acceptance of every manifestation as God-sent? What has been your experience of such manifestations of the Spirit? How would you say that you and your congregation interact with spiritual gifts (for example, stifling, using with discernment, dangerously overindulging without discernment)?

Paul's Farewell
Read 1 Thessalonians 5:23-28

Paul tended to conclude his letters in a liturgical manner, whether a blessing pronounced upon the audience (as in 1 Thessalonians 5:23-24; see also Galatians 6:16; Ephesians 6:23; 2 Thessalonians 3:16) or a doxology glorifying God (Romans 16:25-27; Philippians 4:20). Paul almost always concluded with a prayer wish for the favor of Christ to rest on the congregation (1 Thessalonians 5:28; 1 Corinthians 16:23; 2 Corinthians 13:13; Galatians 6:18; Ephesians 6:24; Philippians 4:23; Colossians 4:18; 2 Thessalonians 3:18; Philemon 25). This reflected the natural setting for the reading of these letters—the worship gathering—of which Paul was quite aware as he wrote. Indeed, Paul solemnly commanded that the letter be read not just by a select few in Thessalonica but to all believers (1 Thessalonians 5:27).

Paul was concerned to safeguard against the text being used selectively by a coterie of leaders, insisting rather that it be made directly available to the whole congregation. Later in history, such a concern would infuse the Reformation leaders' commitment to getting the Scriptures out to the people, to the "whole church," so as to free the text from being used selectively by a clergy class. Making the text "public" has the effect of rendering all accountable to the Word rather than allowing some to subordinate the Word to their own ends and agendas.

Paul's benediction strategically recalled themes from earlier parts of the letter. First, God's desire that the believers be "sanctified" (1 Thessalonians 5:23) recalled 4:1-8, where the theme of becoming holy in conformity to God's will was developed particularly with regard to the "body." Second, the benediction highlighted the "coming of our Lord," a recurring motif of the letter (1:10; 2:19; 3:13; 4:15-17; 5:2-5). Third, Paul prayed for the believers to be preserved in that day, which recalled the earlier benediction (3:13) as well as the ethical exhortations to be prepared for that day (5:6-11). Paul thus left the hearers with these important themes ringing in their ears as the letter was rolled up and put away.

PAUL'S FAREWELL

• How would the liturgical, worshipful setting have affected the reading and hearing of this letter? Why was it important to Paul that his words be passed on directly to all the believers, rather than indirectly through the local leaders? How would it benefit your congregation to increase people's direct exposure to the words and world of the Scriptures?

• Review how the topics of sanctification and preparedness for the Lord's coming were developed throughout the letter. How would a special focus on these topics equip the believers to persevere in faithful discipleship?

IN CLOSING

• What has been the most valuable insight you have gained in your study of this letter? How will that insight shape your life in the days and weeks to come? What is the most urgent challenge you have heard as you studied? How will you respond to that challenge?

• Pray for God's guidance and help to take to heart the insights and challenges God has given you. (In a group setting, you may desire to pray for one another in this regard.)

• Close with the assurance that Paul himself gives in 1 Thessalonians 5:24.

IV THE DAY OF THE LORD

The Situation Behind Second Thessalonians
Read 2 Thessalonians 1:3-4; 2:1-8; 3:6

During the past two centuries, biblical scholars have called into question the authorship of Second Thessalonians based both on similarities and dissimilarities with First Thessalonians. The two letters do have a remarkably similar outline, particularly with regard to the more formal features (the letter openings, the double thanksgivings, and the double benedictions). They also move from addressing the conditions of persecution to eschatological topics to matters of church life. Alongside these similarities, however, are noteworthy differences in writing style and in the sense of emotional connection between writer and addressees (First Thessalonians is much more expressive than the more formal Second Thessalonians.). Some have also suggested that the eschatological viewpoints—the expectation of the sudden appearing of the Lord in First Thessalonians and the expectation that the Second Coming will be preceded by signs one can discern in advance—are incompatible.

Many respected scholars interpret Second Thessalonians as a letter written by a disciple of Paul, using First Thessalonians as a model, to address a new situation in one or more Christian churches (not necessarily in Thessalonica) using the deceased apostle's authority.

Second Thessalonians 2:2 is indeed taken as a sign that pseudonymous letters (letters attributed to a famous and respected author) had already begun to be circulated in the apostle's name. Pseudonymous writing was regarded more as a sign of respect and a means by which to connect one's work with an established tradition than as an act of deception and forgery. It would be a stretch of the convention, however, to write in the name of a recently deceased figure rather than in the name of a figure from the "classical" past.

Other scholars still read the letter as essentially Paul's own communication. If we take seriously the identical, collegial authorship of these letters, we might find a ready explanation for differences in style and vocabulary. Paul certainly wrote First Thessalonians; the "I" of 2:18–3:5 and his own personality and feelings emerge more forcefully there. After discussion of the pastoral concerns calling for Second Thesslonians, the actual writing may have been left to Silvanus or to Timothy, whose style differed from Paul's own, with Paul adding his authenticating signature in 2 Thessalonians 3:17-18.

The eschatological perspectives of the two letters, moreover, stand side-by-side elsewhere in the New Testament. Mark 13, for example, presents Jesus' teaching on signs that would precede his return in glory together with the warning that this coming would be sudden and unexpected. The juxtaposition of Mark 13:28-31 and 13:32-37 is especially striking, the first asserting that by careful observation of these signs the disciples will know that the Son of Man is near, the second cautioning them that "about that day or hour no one knows" save the Father.

Those who read Second Thessalonians as an authentic Pauline letter see it as responding to a later development in the Thessalonian church. Some think that only a brief amount of time had passed since the writing of First Thessalonians, given the similarities in form and topics between the two letters. Others allow for more than a few months, all the more as Paul and his team would have continued to maintain a relationship with that church (visiting, receiving news) until his arrest in Jerusalem and might easily have kept a copy of his earlier letter to that church for reference. A few scholars, however, read Second Thessalonians as prior to First Thessalonians, addressing an earlier and more heated stage in the experience of persecution.

Choosing between these options is far from simple. Whatever one decides, however, it is clear that Second Thessalonians addressed three principal concerns. Paul worked to equip believers to endure in their commitment to Christ in the face of hostility and heavy pressure from outside. Second, he corrected a view of the end times that had collapsed the futurity of Jesus' return into the present, preparing the believers to face ongoing trials as the mystery of lawlessness continued to work and come to a head. Third, Second Thessalonians instructed the church to act together to correct the behavior of some Christians who, believing the end to be here, had abandoned their productive occupations and were living off the charity of the community.

THE SITUATION BEHIND SECOND THESSALONIANS

• What are the three main proposals regarding how Second Thessalonians fits into the Pauline mission? Which seem possible to you? Which of these proposals makes the most sense to you? How will you read Second Thessalonians in light of these discussions?

• Read Mark 13, 1 Thessalonians 5:1-6, and 2 Thessalonians 2:3-8. How were Christians able to hold together the belief that (a) certain signs would precede and therefore signal the end and (b) the return of Christ would be sudden, catching people off guard? How might each facet promote discipleship and aid commitment to following Jesus?
• What were the three main issues this letter addressed? Which of these issues resonate with conditions in your local church, your denomination, or the global church?

A Strange Claim to Honor
Read 2 Thessalonians 1:1-12

The opening of the letter once more gives us a window into a Christian community's experience of being rejected, shamed, and abused by its non-Christian society. Indeed, these persecutions were being endured at the time of the letter's writing (2 Thessalonians 1:4, 5). The writers were thus keenly aware that they needed to help their converts regard persevering in the face of hostility as advantageous and ennobling. Their non-Christian neighbors wanted the converts to see their departure from the dominant culture's way of life as disadvantageous and shameful to them, so as to win them back.

According to Second Thessalonians, the people on the "outside" of the Christian group are also on the "outside" of God's favor and approval. These people neither know God nor obey God, particularly as God's will has been revealed in the gospel (2 Thessalonians 1:8), with the result that they are themselves a dishonorable lot (lacking both in piety and justice, since they flout God's commands). Indeed, the very pressures they apply to the believers in an attempt to shame them into conformity with the dominant culture's values necessitate God's visitation of judgment on their heads. Those pressures and persecutions are thereby declared undeserved and unjust, with the result that the believers are encouraged to withstand them, assured of God's approval of their walk and of God's vindication of their honor against the outsiders. God's court issues the only verdict—the only estimation of who is honorable and who is censurable—worth considering, since God's opinion confers eternal honor or eternal disgrace.

The writers praised the converts for bravely enduring attack from outside, reporting that they were spreading the good word about the converts' noble character throughout the churches of God (2 Thessalonians1:3-4). In particular, their reliability and love in their relationships with one another, even while under attack, was held up as an important contribution to the noble estimation God and the churches had formed of them (1:3). In short, they were doing everything "right" in God's eyes, which would come as a powerful encouragement, since society had been trying to convince them they had been doing everything "wrong."

The writers also ennobled the experience of persecution itself, however. They saw it as a sign of God's just judgment and as the means by which believers were fitted for God's kingdom itself (2 Thessalonians 1:5), a theme steeped in Jewish tradition as well (see Wisdom of Solomon 3:4-5). Through this hardship, God would shape (not shame) them, demonstrating their worth, with the result that they would enter into God's reward. No longer would they be concerned with their lost honor in the world's eyes or with escaping the heat but rather with proving themselves worthy of a greater honor (1:5, 11). In this way, any temporal ambitions were defused and the human trait of "ambition" itself harnessed to help believers persevere for eternal honor.

   In what way, though, was the believers' suffering a "sign" or "proof" of God's righteous judgment? Did the writers think that the persecutions came upon the believers because God judged the converts worthy of punishment? The letter's own logic in 1:6-7, which explains God's justice, leads us away from such a reading. In light of those verses, the believers' suffering was really a sign or proof of God's imminent vindication (positive judgment) of the believers and punishment (negative judgment) of those who afflicted the innocent righteous. This, too, was a familiar topic in Jewish literature on suffering for righteousness or God's law (see 4 Maccabees 9–12). Because God is just, the unjust affliction of the converts was evidence that God's judgment would soon break in to set matters right.

A STRANGE CLAIM TO HONOR

• Who constitutes your "court of reputation"? Do you seek to have standing and prestige in the eyes of "society"? How does this affect your goals; your priorities; your choices; your investments of energy, material resources, and time? To what extent do you seek to have God's approval and esteem? Reflect on one or two particular instances when this goal ran counter to gaining approval from peers. Which did you choose, and why?

• How do the writers ennoble the experience of persecution for the sake of Christ? Why was it important for the converts that their leaders engaged in such reinterpretation of society's hostility and rejection? How would the conviction that God is just help the converts persevere?

• Talking about how God is at work through suffering and hardship can lead to the misperception of God as an abusive parent who is behind all human evil and misery. What specific kinds of suffering was Second Thessalonians addressing and interpreting in 1:3-12? To what situations can this interpretation safely and responsibly be applied for Christians in your context? What kinds of suffering were not clearly in the writers'

minds and therefore were not addressed by these topics? Why is it important to make these distinctions?
• Persecution of Christians is not a thing of the past, especially outside the United States. How does the response in 2 Thessalonians 1:3-12 (perhaps especially 1:3-4) begin to suggest ways in which you can encourage the believers in other lands?

The Mystery of Lawlessness
Read 2 Thessalonians 2:1-12

With the second chapter, the writers move to their second concern, namely, the correction of a potential misunderstanding of Christian eschatology (end-time expectation). The day of the Lord has not yet arrived (2 Thessalonians 2:1-2), even though it may well be very near. On the one hand, the writers want to affirm the certainty of Christ's return and the reward of the righteous; but, on the other hand, they also want to affirm its futurity. That is, it is indeed coming; but it is not yet here. As proof, the writers revisit the basic end-time schedule of events that they share, to a large extent, with other Jewish apocalyptic groups. Before the end, there will be a widespread revolt against God's order and standards and the emergence of a figure in whom the human and demonic revolt against God comes to fullest and final expression: "the lawless one" (2:3).

At present, the "mystery of lawlessness" is already at work, noticeably in the rejection of the gospel and in the persecution of the believers. There is, however, an unnamed restraining force or restrainer (2 Thessalonians 2:6-7) holding back the lawless one; but the coming of the lawless one cannot be far away. In the widespread rejection of the gospel and the followers of Christ, which is the result of Satan's deceptions, a person can already see the signs of the lawless one's appearance (2:9-10). Nevertheless, the end of the sequence is the same: The lawless one and all who have been duped by Satan fall under God's condemnation and perish at Christ's appearing (2:8, 11-12).

This passage introduces a number of important "unknowns" into our interpretation of the letter. Who is the lawless one? Who and/or what is restraining him? With regard to the former, Jewish and Christian apocalypses tended to look ahead to a single person or event in which all the evil and ungodliness now at work in the world, mostly under the surface and frustratingly elusive, would come to full and open expression. The Jews had witnessed many prototypes of such a person, as a line of Gentile overlords (Nebuchadnezzar, Antiochus IV, Pompey, Caligula) either desecrated or threatened to desecrate what was most holy and symbolically important — the Temple of God in Jerusalem. These figures entered apocalyptic lore as early as Daniel 7–8 and continued to be seen somewhat impersonally in Mark 13:14 and very personally in Revelation 13. The lawless one is but another cast from the same mold. (Note the emphasis in 2 Thessalonians 2:4 on his actions against acknowledged gods and places of worship.) This figure is but another way of expressing this conviction that the enemy of God and God's people will finally come out into the open — only to be destroyed once and for all.

The "restraining power," which is referred to both as an impersonal force and as a personal agent in this passage, is far less clear. The best suggestion for what the writers had in mind by this is the Roman Empire and her emperor which, despite their faults, nevertheless maintained order and prevented lawlessness from running amok. The writers, however, may also have had in mind some angelic power, since such powers are often depicted as exercising a restraining role in apocalypses (whether holding back the elements of judgment or controlling the gate of the abyss; see Revelation 7:1-3; 9:1-3; 20:1-3). The converts were thus reminded that they were witnessing—and participating in—the opening acts of the end-time drama. The coming of Christ remained imminent, which rendered the rebellion and advent of the lawless one all the more imminent; but they were still living out the "beginning of the birth pangs" (Mark 13:8).

THE MYSTERY OF LAWLESSNESS

• Read 2 Thessalonians 2:1-12 carefully, working out the "order" of end-time events discussed in that passage. Read Mark 13 and Daniel 7. In what ways does the Pauline tradition resemble the Jewish apocalyptic tradition as represented by Daniel and Jesus? In what ways are the emphases different in these traditions?

• Even though the lawless one may be seen as a fearsome figure, what are the indications in the text that God is in control from beginning to end, that the lawless one is never a real threat to God's order? Why would it be important for the converts in the midst of their current experiences to know this?

• What does the passage say about the "here and now" of the converts? If the revelation of the lawless one is still in the future, where are God's enemies at work in the present?

The Deceived and the Enlightened
Read 2 Thessalonians 2:1-15

We need to step back from the actual content of the passage, which all too easily leads to rather futile end-times speculation and games of "pin the tail on the

Antichrist," and observe how the passage shaped the out-
look of the converts who heard it. That is to say, alongside
contemplating the eschatological content, we need to
attend to its rhetorical function and social effect in the situation being addressed. Apocalypses and discussion of
apocalyptic topics often have as their goal the clarification
of the cosmic significance of the choices and alliances one
makes in the here and now. While speaking of future and
otherworldly realities, these apocalypses also shape the
hearer's perception of present, this-worldly realities.

What the lawless one would bring out in full force
openly in the future was already at work behind the
scenes, namely the "mystery of lawlessness." At the same
time, the lawless one was at work trying to block people
from seeing the truth and from embracing the salvation
that God has announced. Who were the deceived? The
converts would immediately see their non-Christian neighbors—the very people trying to harass and shame them
from continuing in their Christian walk—as the targets
and victims of the lawless one's deceptions. The non-
Christians' rejection of the gospel and their assault on the
believers was part of the working of the "mystery of lawlessness" already active in the present time of the hearers,
the beginnings of the final "rebellion" against God.

Nevertheless, it was the persecutors who, although acting and no doubt thinking of themselves as the powerful
guardians of traditional values, were actually caught in the
lawless one's delusion and were spiraling downward to
the abyss without even realizing their danger and doom.
They were not, however, merely victims. In choosing
against the gospel, they had refused to accept God's truth
and had clung to disobedience as their preferred lifestyle
(2 Thessalonians 2:11-12). Therefore, they not only came

under the lawless one's sway but God also sealed their doom by giving them over wholly to that delusion.

The believers, however, were in a privileged position— even while they were being persecuted! They had received the necessary information to avoid falling prey to the lawless one's deceptions (2 Thessalonians 2:3, 15). Standing firm in the face of societal pressure and holding on to the authentic message of Paul and his team emerged as the course of action that kept one safe from falling prey to this global deception (2:9-12). Doing this leads to deliverance and the fulfillment of God's good purposes for the converts (2:13), which includes obtaining a share in the honor that Jesus himself enjoys (2:14).

The NRSV rightly ends the section that began at 2:1 with 2:15, which returns to the words "by word" and "by our letter" (compare 2:2 and 2:15). The writers have used a literary device called *inclusio*. The use of this literary device is important because it tells us that the thanksgiving in 2:13 does not begin a new section. Instead, it completes the current section, highlighting once again the contrast between the converts (2:13-15) and those outside the church (2:9-12) so that those inside will not be tempted to revert to the lifestyle and worldview of those outside.

THE DECEIVED AND THE ENLIGHTENED

• What is the destiny of converts in the eschatological scheme the writers of 2 Thessalonians 2:1-15 developed? What is the role of the theme of "delusion" in the depiction of the dangers of not knowing God and obeying the gospel? How will the converts think differently about their experience of being persecuted and about their neighbors who are reproaching them for turning away from idols to serve the one God?

• How do apocalyptic topics (discussion about the end times or the Second Coming) in 1 Thessalonians 5 and 2 Thessalonians 2 change the way the believers respond to the challenges in the here and now? Reflect on your own engagement with the eschatology of the church (for example, your appreciation of the Second Coming, your reading of such texts as Revelation). In what ways and to what extent have these topics enhanced your commitment to Christ, to mission, and to authentic discipleship?

• The writers have been speaking in very stark terms about insiders and outsiders and in a manner most uncongenial to our modern, pluralistic environment. In what ways might the pastoral needs of the historical situation call for (and justify) such stark contrasts? To what extent are we to maintain this distinction between those who follow the gospel and those who devote themselves to some other way of life, so as not to sacrifice our witness to Jesus on the altar of pluralism? How do we temper it so as to avoid the opposite dangers of religious fanaticism and exclusivity?

The Partnership of Prayer
Read 2 Thessalonians 2:16–3:5

The writers effected a transition between major topics (the futurity of the day of the Lord and the problem of the "idle" in the Christian community) by expressing their prayers for the converts and their requests for prayer in their behalf. Prayer—holding up one another in the presence of God and seeking God's timely and specific favors for one another—was a primary sign of partnership and medium of pastoral care in the early church. A simple concordance search of Pauline letters clearly shows the importance of prayer for the maturing of disciples, the spreading of the gospel, and the safety and success of the missionaries. Prayer was regarded, moreover, as effective. It was not a pious act of vague well wishing but a way of securing tangible and timely aid from the Almighty for one another.

Praying for the congregation, the writers called attention to the "eternal encouragement" ("Comfort" may be too weak a translation here.) and reliable, bright hope that God had given them (2 Thessalonians 2:16). These gifts of God would enable the converts to keep swimming against the tide of their society, since they had God's strength and the assurance of a greater future. In a second prayer, the writers prayed that the Lord would focus their hearts upon God's love for them and upon Christ's steadfast endurance (3:5). These topics were closely associated with the cross of Jesus, the supreme manifestation of God's love and Christ's steadfastness, which was likely to come to the forefront of the converts' minds as well. As their attention was fixed on this costliest of gifts, the converts would be motivated to persevere out of gratitude to God and to Christ, to make an honorable return of grace for grace rather than turn away or give up on account of the pressure from outside. The theme that connects both prayers is the confidence that God was at work in the converts. It was God who would establish them in the way of salvation (2:16). It was the Lord who supported their obedience to the apostolic tradition (3:4). It was the Lord who protected the converts from the evil one (3:3), whose activity was a prominent topic in 2:3-12.

The apostle's team needed prayer as well, however; and so prayer became an act of mutual caring and encouragement. First, they asked for prayers for the success of their preaching, choosing a very vivid metaphor: They wanted to see the Lord's word "run" or "spread rapidly" (2 Thessalonians 3:1). The unimpeded progress of the word needs also to be met by the open reception of the word for what it is — God's glorious message of deliverance. But the team also faced opposition and so asked for prayers for deliverance from those who would not respond in "faith" (3:2) but rather would cling to their "wicked and evil" character and hinder the missionaries. The writers chose to describe the opponents of their work as *atopoi*, which means "out of place," thus turning back on their own heads the non-Christians' view of the Christians as "out of place," as deviants requiring correction.

THE PARTNERSHIP OF PRAYER

• Using a concordance and a Bible, look up the occurrences of the words *pray, prayer, prayers,* and *praying* in letters attributed to Paul. Reflect also on the specific prayers in Second Thessalonians. What kinds of favors did Paul seek from God for his converts? What help did Paul ask his prayer partners to seek on his behalf? How did he envision prayer working within the life of a local congregation? What guidance do these examples provide for you in your own prayer life and your participation in the prayers of the congregation?
• How fully do your own investments of yourself reflect the "good hope" that God has given us? To what extent does your life reveal a heart fixed on the generosity and steadfastness God has shown us in Christ? How would you pray to grow in these areas?

The Healing Power of Shame
Read 2 Thessalonians 3:6-18

The third concern guiding the writers was the report that some converts were "living in idleness" (2 Thessalonians 3:6). The Greek adverb translated "in idleness" may also be rendered "in an unruly or undisciplined manner." Unfortunately, we have little information on why these believers were not engaged in fruitful labor. Were they unemployed persons who were attracted to the gospel but who then continued to live off the charity of the community? Were they formerly employed persons who came to believe that the closeness of the "end" meant that the ordinary business and rules of life no longer mattered, so these people stopped working? Were they workers shunned by the non-believing community and thus driven out of work? Were they self-appointed spiritual directors of the community who gave up their mundane occupations so as to devote themselves full time to regulating the lives (that is, meddling, being busybodies) of their less spiritual sisters and brothers?

Certainty on this matter eludes us, but the writers' response was clear enough. Part of the "tradition" the converts received from Paul was not just instruction from his lips but instruction from his example. This was in keeping with the tradition of Greco-Roman philosophers who sought to teach not only by word but also by example how to live a life of virtue. Paul's example taught that it was noble that one work to support oneself and one's God-given mission (2 Thessalonians 3:7-8; see 1 Thessalonians 2:9-10); his explicit command taught that it was necessary (2 Thessalonians 3:10). Of course, Paul and his team would be the first to encourage charity toward those who were unable to support themselves or whose circumstances had forced them into want (as in his collection for the poor in Judea). But to abuse charity to support an ignoble and idle lifestyle went beyond the pale, dishonoring charity itself. The writers asserted that they worked with their own hands even though they had the authority as apostles to receive community support (3:8-9; see 1 Corinthians 9:1-18), so important was it to them that their example should encourage all to persevere in profitable labor.

The writers were concerned that outsiders could legitimately censure the Christian community on this point.

The idle could quickly become the disruptive, the unruly, even the rebellious; and the church could not afford to be seen to promote this. Another concern was that the limited resources of the community for legitimate relief would be drained needlessly by such idlers, rather than be multiplied by the work and contributions of every believer who was doing good (that is, bringing relief to those in genuine need). The writers relied not only on their authority but also on community support to enforce their values.

The writers called the group to shame the idlers into shaping up (2 Thessalonians 3:6, 14-15). By withholding fellowship (3:6, 14) — but all in a spirit of correction and love (3:15) — they were to communicate that the idlers' way of life was not something the community would affirm or tolerate. The idlers, ideally, would feel shame before their sisters and brothers and, seeking to regain the respect of their fellow Christians, would fall in line with the apostle's example.

THE HEALING POWER OF SHAME

• Why were the writers concerned about "idlers" in the congregation? Why did the writers want them to return to productive labor? How would the church reinforce their instructions?

• The apostles taught by word and by personal example. What does your personal example teach? Is it fully consonant with what you would advise or teach others by word? For example, if you want to emphasize the importance of evangelism or working for social justice, does your own example reflect and model these emphases? What do you need to change to bring your example more fully in line with the values and beliefs you hold dear?

• The Christian community was an important force in encouraging individual believers to engage in behaviors consonant with the new life and to desist from behaviors that were not in line with the gospel (see also Matthew 18:15-20; Galatians 6:1; James 5:19-20). To what extent do fellow Christians continue to exercise this ministry of reinforcement in your local congregation? To what extent have fellow Christians abdicated their responsibility to help one another pursue what is noble and avoid what is sinful? What factors might feed into this (that is, privatization of religion, lack of agreement on what behaviors are and are not consonant with the gospel)? How far should a congregation go toward exercising a positive but directive influence on the way of life of each of its members?

IN CLOSING

• Second Thessalonians has invited us to explore many challenging issues. Which discussions have been most thought provoking for you? How has your view of discipleship or of living together as the church changed, or at least been stretched? What one thing do you take away from this study as God's instructions or encouragement to you?

• Pray for your fellow Christians, for your pastoral staff, for your congregation's missionaries; and close with the benediction prayer of 2 Thessalonians 3:16.

V THE BELOVED SAINTS IN PHILIPPI

The Pastoral Needs at Philippi
Read Philippians 1:12-14; 1:27–2:5; 2:25-30; 3:17–4:3; 4:10-20

While First Thessalonians (and perhaps Second Thessalonians) represents one of Paul's earliest surviving letters, Philippians is quite possibly one of the apostle's latest letters. The Letter to the Philippians is extremely difficult to date with certainty. In it, Paul reveals that he is a prisoner; but he does not say where he is in bonds (Philippians 1:7, 17). He was most likely imprisoned in Rome, which would put the letter between A.D. 60 and 62. "The whole imperial guard" (1:13) and "the emperor's household" (4:22) were in Rome. Paul was "imprisoned" under house arrest, awaiting a verdict of life or death (1:12-13, 19-26). The distance from Philippi to Rome was daunting; but Paul was a prisoner in Rome for two years, and the Philippians were friends of the sort who would put themselves out for Paul. Two other possible locations for the writing of Philippians are Caesarea, where Paul was imprisoned between 58 and 60, and Ephesus, where he faced severe trials that might have included imprisonment on a capital charge (see 1 Corinthians 15:32; 2 Corinthians 1:8-10). The latter locale would put the writing of the letter closer to 55 or 56.

Paul wrote to a congregation that held a special place

in his heart. This was the only church that he addressed as his "partners" (the deeper sense of the Greek words rendered "sharing" and "share" in Philippians 1:5, 7; see also 4:15-16), both in salvation and in the propagation of the gospel. This was the one church from which Paul accepted money for support of himself and his missionary endeavors. Whenever Paul mentioned the Macedonian churches, he did so with gratitude and praise (see 2 Corinthians 8:1-5). Three of the topics Paul addressed in Philippians related directly to the Philippian Christians' partnership with him. First (or last, in the order of writing), Paul thanked them for the material support they sent him through Epaphroditus during his confinement (Philippians 4:10-20). Second, Paul eased their concern over the well-being of Epaphroditus, their emissary of mercy, who they heard fell ill on his mission (2:25-30). Third, Paul provided them with an update on his own situation (1:12-26).

At the same time, Paul, having learned something of the Philippians' state from Epaphroditus, addressed two facets of their situation. First, he wanted two leading figures in the life of the church, Euodia and Syntyche, to reconcile (Philippians 4:2-3). Their divisive quarrel (about which we will never know details, thanks to Paul's discretion) threatened the primary value of the Christian family: harmony and unity (2:1-4). Paul was therefore also concerned to calm any ripples of rivalry or division that might have been moving out from these two leaders into the larger congregation. This was all the more urgent in light of the other concern: the Philippian Christians' continued strength and perseverance in the face of their neighbors' hostility toward the group and its alternative to the Roman peace (1:27-30).

THE PASTORAL NEEDS AT PHILIPPI

• Philippians has often been described as a "letter of friendship." Read through Philippians and note where the topics of partnership, of mutual concern, of gift exchange, and of common values emerge. What would be the purpose of passages talking about enemies (Philippians 1:28; 3:2-3, 18-19) in a letter of friendship?

• Imagine Paul as he sat down to write to the Philippian church. He listed all the things to which he wanted to respond as well as the concerns he wished to address. After reading Philippians, what would you surmise was on that list?

• In what ways does your church relate most deeply to the church in Philippi (in concern for missionary partners, in dissonance within the congregation, in hostile opposition from non-Christians)? How do you hope your study of Philippians will equip you to build up your congregation in this area?

Partners in the Gospel
Read Philippians 1:1-11

Paul speaks of the church in Philippi as a source of constant refreshment for his heart and his mission. The affective language in the thanksgiving section (Philippians 1:3-8) is remarkable. Every time the Philippian Christians crossed his memory, Paul found cause to thank God; every time Paul prayed for that church, it was with joy in his heart (1:3-4). Such could not have been said about the churches in Galatia or in Corinth. For significant stretches of time, Paul would have felt a stab of pain or anxiety when they crossed his mind or when he prayed for their establishment in the one gospel. Paul's relationship with the Philippians was a harbor for the apostle, a safe place.

When we think about the missionary braving dangers and hardships and preaching courageously in the face of opposition, we should remember that Christians like those in Philippi were present with him in his heart. They gave him both the inner encouragement mentioned in Philippians 1:3-4 and the physical signs of partnership alluded to in 1:7 and referred to more precisely in 2:25 and 4:10-20.

The Philippian Christians were "sharers in grace" with Paul (1:7), both as he labored for the gospel and as he languished in chains. The NRSV tries to clarify the Greek by adding the word "God's" before "grace," but this may obscure the point. People formed "grace" relationships throughout their lives with friends, patrons, and clients (the realms of social interaction in the ancient world where "grace" language was at home). Paul may have been acknowledging here the importance of the "grace" relationship he had with his friends in Philippi in all aspects of his missionary endeavors.

When we compare Paul's relationship with the Philippian Christians to that with the Corinthian Christians, the depth of mutual trust and affection that marked the former relationship becomes clearer. Paul's acceptance of monetary support from the Philippians was not just a sign of their devotion to the apostle. It was also a sign of the apostle's confidence in the church that they would not use gift giving as leverage on him. Paul dared not accept money from the Corinthian Christians, since he sensed (and rightly so) that the patrons in the church would misinterpret and exploit such gift giving.

Paul concluded the letter's opening by sharing the content of his prayer for the church. That is, he prayed that their love would continue to be combined with the God-given knowledge and insight that enables discernment of what is essential (*ta diapheronta*) to being found sincere and blameless at the last day (Philippians 1:9-11). The Greek word in the preceding paraphrase is rendered as "what is best" in the NRSV, but this is not precisely its meaning. Its opposite is *adiapheronta* or *adiaphera*—the things that do not matter, about which Christians should be tolerant and not become divisive or intolerant.

Love, coupled with a focus on what really matters for producing the righteous fruit for which Jesus will look in each Christian and in the church as a whole, is presented up front as a remedy for the main problem facing the congregation. That problem was the polarization of leading figures (see Philippians 4:2-3) over what was no doubt an indifferent matter viewed from the perspective of Christ's judgment seat. Paul also knew how pride, posturing, and competition could take hold in such disagreements, blighting the harmony of a church (2:1-11). His prayer for love coupled with insight into what really matters, therefore, was quite apt.

PARTNERS IN THE GOSPEL

• Reflect on the triumphs and trials of Paul's missionary work. Why would a congregation like the one in Philippi be such a source of internal comfort and joy? In what ways did the Philippian Christians contribute to Paul's ongoing success as a missionary and to his faithfulness while a prisoner? How did Paul continue to contribute to the Philippian Christians' growth and health as a body of disciples?

• Is your church involved in a partnership with a missionary or campus minister or other person engaged in ministry beyond your congregational setting? In what ways has that partnership been more than a financial commitment? How have parishioners been personally and prayerfully involved in supporting that ministry? Has your church been a source of refreshment and a safe place for the minister's heart? If you have not been involved, what might motivate you to seek such a relationship? In what ways could you partner without adding financial cost?

• Prayerfully reflect on standing at the judgment seat of Christ (see 2 Corinthians 5:9-10 for a focusing Scripture). As you look back on your life, what do you see to have mattered in the light of this day? In what have you invested yourself that will not ultimately matter? How can these reflections help you refocus your energies in the present?

• Are there disagreements between members of your church over issues that are not essential to being found sincere and blameless on the day of Christ? Are you personally involved in such a disagreement? How can you and your fellow believers get a better view of the importance of these issues and let love and insight restore harmony?

Sibling Rivalry
Read Philippians 1:12-26

Paul reported on his current condition, a matter of concern to his friends in Philippi. He was imprisoned, perhaps literally chained to a Roman soldier; under house arrest (or in a prison facility, if not in Rome); and awaiting the outcome of a trial the verdict of which would mean life or death. Paul held up one aspect of his situation for special consideration. While he was imprisoned and "off the circuit," as it were, other preachers had sought to distinguish themselves in spreading the gospel (most probably in Rome itself). Paul considered that some did this out of a sincere heart for God; but he knew that others did it out of a sense of rivalry with Paul, trying to replace him in the limelight of the churches. Thinking that Paul had the same spirit of reputation-seeking that they had, the rivals believed their activity would grieve Paul as he watched others increase in fame at his expense (Philippians 1:17).

Paul did not respond, however, as these rivals expected. He was not drawn into a spirit of rivalry and competition on account of what other people were doing but rather set his eyes on what the Lord was doing. Paul saw that, whatever people's motives, the gospel was spreading even more since his imprisonment; and that was his only concern. The rivals were brought in as negative examples, embodying strife, rivalry, and selfish ambition—living as "enemies of the cross," in a sense. Paul thus had an opportunity to show how a "friend of the cross" responds to such people: Rising above partisanship and concern for his own standing, he discerned what really mattered in the situation and so rejoiced in the Lord (Philippians 1:18). One should suspect that Paul introduced these examples to help the Christians in Philippi deal as maturely with the emergence of rivalry and selfish conceit in their midst.

SIBLING RIVALRY

• Why would Paul's imprisonment embolden other Christians in Rome to take up the preaching of the gospel? What would those people, motivated by envy, rivalry, and selfish ambition, hope to achieve by preaching the gospel? How might Paul have been able to tell if their efforts were sincere? How might the Thessalonian congregation? When, if ever, have these factors polluted your own service in the church or in ministry beyond the church?

• What does Paul's example teach about how a Christian is to respond to her or his rivals? Have you ever been able, or do you currently have an opportunity, to put this into practice?

Death Is a Door
Re-read Philippians 1:12-26

In Paul's attitude while imprisoned and in the shadow of death, we find the pinnacle of confidence in and devotion to the Lord. Paul defined his life as an opportunity to serve God (Philippians 1:22). He did not demand comfort or safety but sought only that the word of the Lord would spread as a result of his life and that Christ would be honored, whether in Paul's continued existence or in his execution (1:20). For this reason, Paul could accept his circumstances with a confident and uncomplaining heart. His confinement emboldened the witness of other Christians; and for that reason he did not chafe at his chains, though they no doubt chafed on him (1:12-14).

Also remarkable was Paul's confidence in the face of death, which he regarded not as an evil but as the gate through which he would pass to enter the brightness of the presence of the Lord (Philippians 1:23). He did not think of dying as something to be feared or avoided but as "gain" (1:21).

Early Christian leaders were well aware of the power that the "fear of death" had in the lives of the people around them. The writer of Hebrews regarded the fear of death as the means by which Satan kept people enslaved (Hebrews 2:14-15). Greco-Roman philosophers likewise recognized the fear of death as a great impediment to freedom. The person who feared imprisonment or death gave away his or her freedom to whoever had the power to imprison or kill. How could one be sure that one would always act in accordance with virtue and one's conscience in such circumstances?

Paul found that freedom in his single-hearted dedication to serve the Lord, whose love filled his life and heart (see Galatians 2:20). Since the aim of his life was serving Jesus, whatever untoward circumstances Paul encountered were not a hindrance to his finding meaning in his life or a threat to his fulfillment of his deepest desires and wishes. It is only the person who can say, "for me, to live means Christ" who can also say, "to die means gain."

DEATH IS A DOOR

• Reflect on Paul's life choices, the activity that occupied his entire adult life, and the experiences of Christ that he personally enjoyed. To what extent could Paul rightly say that, for him, "Living is Christ" (Philippians 1:21) or "The life I now live in the flesh I live by faith in the Son of God" (Galatians 2:20)? Why did this sense of living with and for Christ give Paul peace in the face of death?

• Tell a story about the life (and death) of someone who inspired you to embrace a godly life more completely. What was compelling about the person?

• How do you set the goals and priorities in your life? Paul apparently did not have an immediate family to support, and thus may have seemed freer to engage in a single-minded life for Christ. Does God call everyone to such a life? How can you tell?

• Clearly Christ is important to you, since you are undertaking this study of God's Word. What other things are important to you in your life? What do you want to get out of life before you die? To what extent would it be true for you to say, "To live means Christ"? Does your own death threaten your enjoyment or achievement of what is important to you; or have you come to a place in your life where you, too, can look at death with the same confidence Paul did?

Triumphant Witness
Read Philippians 1:27-30

For both the Thessalonians and the Philippians, the confession of Jesus as "Lord" and "Savior" and the expectation that he would come as king brought Christians into conflict with their neighbors because they lived in a context where Augustus and his successors were already lauded with those very titles. The difference in the situation Philippians addressed was that the addressees had been Christians for at least six years by this time, and possibly as long as ten to twelve, so that this hostility was not a new reality for them.

For Paul it was of utmost importance that his friends in

Philippi match hostility from outside with internal unity, support, encouragement, and aid. If harmony and unity were to erode from within, the assaults from without would stand a better chance of achieving their objective: wearing down the "deviants" and bringing them back into conformity with "good Roman values." Paul wanted the Philippians to remain strong so that they could maintain their witness of courageous perseverance. As they faced off with an unbelieving world, unafraid and unshaken, they testified with a voice more eloquent than words that Christ is worth everything and that God—and God's judgment— is real. In such a way, endurance of persecution would become a proclamation of God's triumph over the world.

TRIUMPHANT WITNESS

• Review the reasons the majority of the citizens of Philippi would have responded negatively to the gospel of Jesus the Messiah and to those who embraced that gospel. Why would it have been important to the perseverance of each Christian in the faith for the body of Christians to be united and harmonious?

• Paul relied heavily on the power of memory in Philippians 1:27. How has the memory of someone, some experience, or some capability sustained you in a difficult time?

• Paul named the experience of suffering for Jesus a "privilege" (Philippians 1:29); but insults, slander, vandalism, assault, and marginalization are far from pleasant experiences. Why should the endurance of hardships encountered for the sake of Christ be thought of as a privilege? Since Paul did not explain this here, consult the passages where he did (Philippians 3:10-11; Romans 6:3-5; 8:12-17).

Church Politics
Read Philippians 2:1-11

Having already announced his principal concern in Philippians 1:27, Paul now addresses at greater length the topic of harmony within the congregation. On the basis both of the genuineness of their shared religious experience and the desire that they had to keep bringing joy to the heart of their imprisoned partner in the gospel (2:1-2), Paul called the Christians to act as friends of one another, as siblings, and more: as noble citizens of the commonwealth of heaven (see 3:20). English translations have difficulty bringing out the political nuances of Paul's language in 1:27: "Conduct yourselves as citizens (*politeuesthe*) [NRSV says, "Live your life"] in a manner worthy of the gospel of Christ." The cardinal political virtue, as the citizens of Philippi no doubt knew, is unity.

Dio Chrysostom, a statesman and philosopher of the late first century, addressed his native city of Prusa at a time when internal dissension had disturbed its harmony: "If a quarrel arises among yourselves and your enemies taunt you because you have wicked citizens and civil unrest, are you not put to shame? . . . It is a truly noble and profitable thing for one and all alike to have a city show itself of one mind, on terms of friendship with itself and one in feeling" (the author's translation of *Oration* 48.5-6). Paul thus employed familiar topics from ethical discussions of how friends and fellow citizens ought to behave toward one another if their behavior was to be considered honorable.

Paul spoke of the threats to unity in frank terms. One source of danger is "selfish ambition or conceit" (Philippians 2:3). When this takes possession of a person, he or she will aim to increase his or her prestige and standing in a community. If anyone opposes or hinders such a person, the result is a competition in which victory can only be won at the cost of defeating the rival in a zero-sum game. Another threat is self-interest (2:4), considering what will be advantageous to oneself rather than advantageous to the whole community.

Paul's remedy was radical and counter-cultural, then as now. Rather than claiming the recognition that may be one's due or seeking to make oneself greater in the eyes of others, the Christian is summoned to focus on honoring his or her fellow believers. Rather than looking out for one's own interests, one is to consider what is in the interests of the circle of friends that Jesus has called together—indeed in the circle of siblings who have been made relations by Jesus' blood. Competition and rivalry where cooperation and solidarity should exist was regarded as a shameful thing in the ancient world. Paul cautioned his friends not to forget their debts to one another as family, friends, and fellow citizens of heaven.

To drive this point home, Paul brought in a poetic passage celebrating Jesus' demonstration of love and generosity toward humanity. Philippians 2:6-11 is often bracketed as an early Christian hymn that Paul took up into his letter; other scholars consider it an original Pauline composition. The position one takes on this issue makes little difference for the interpretation of these verses and for understanding Paul's strategy.

Jesus refused to use his exalted status as an opportunity for personal gain. Instead, he poured out himself completely for others in obedience to God. The pattern of one who "emptied himself" is a necessary remedy for people who are too full of themselves. Jesus, having a legitimate claim to being given preeminence, did not press that claim but rather put God's will for God's people ahead of any desire for recognition of his own status. How much more should those whom Jesus saved, then, rid themselves of attempts to be acknowledged "first" in the community and cast off all conceit and selfishness!

To have the "mind of Christ," without which one is hardly

a disciple at all, is to set aside our rights, claims, and enti-
tlements in the service of others and in the service of God.
To have the "mind of Christ" is to know that it is not we
who must vindicate ourselves against every perceived
slight or triumph in every argument. It is God who vindi-
cates us at the last day and God who must triumph
in God's church. The mind of Christ is formed in the
believer, however, in day-to-day interactions with
fellow believers—in the often trying and wearing circumstances of committee meetings, choir rehearsals, and
administrative hassles.

CHURCH POLITICS

• What resources from the Philippians' own pre-Christian ethical training did Paul use to promote the value of harmony or unity in the
church? What other motivations did he offer for the pursuit of harmony
at the expense of one's own rising to the top of some intra-church
debate?

• If you are in a study group, take turns calling out the various kinds of
power one can have (personal power, position, reputation, and so on).
How "powerful" are persons who seem to give away power; that is, to
enable others to succeed, to meet their goals, to achieve their best?
What sorts of power do you have at your command? What do you
use? What kind of power seems most in keeping with the way Jesus
Christ wants you to live?

• Sing or say all, or several stanzas, of "All Praise to Thee, for Thou,
O King Divine," which is based on Philippians 2:1-11. What does the
Christ hymn (the musical or the scriptural version) teach us about
Christ's own mind and heart? How do competition, rivalry, precedence
seeking, and posturing in the church run counter to that mind? Why
should they therefore be considered out of place among believers?

• Reflect on several episodes in which you found yourself at odds with
another Christian in your local congregation or in another context of
ministry. Were you fighting for something essential or, in the long run,
something that was indifferent? Did the vices of conceit or self-interest
prolong or heighten the quarrel? How would the mind of Christ have
led you to respond?

Recovering a Right Focus
Read Philippians 2:12-18

Paul expressed confidence that the Philippians would do as he advised, intentionally setting aside any internal squabbles that might have been eroding the peace of the congregation (Philippians 2:12). To aid this, he invited them to refocus their energies on making progress in their own walk of discipleship. This was a matter of great seriousness; Paul suggested it should be accompanied by "fear and trembling." This was not because the outcome was in doubt, since God works together with and through the believer to cultivate that harvest of righteousness, but because this was (and is) the single most important business to which human beings could attend. The topic of Paul's prayer in 1:9-11 thus reemerges in the letter as the believers are called away from divisive distractions back toward the things that matter.

Before leaving the topic of dissension, Paul placed it beneath one more lens, namely, the lens of purity and pollution. (The Greek words rendered "blameless" and "without blemish" also figure prominently in discussions of clean and unclean animals and persons.) Both Jews and Gentiles had pollution taboos and purity codes, with the result that Paul's language would be equally effective for both. Murmuring against one's fellow believers and engaging in controversies are diagnosed as defilement of the congregation. (The Greek word recalls the grumbling of the Israelites against Moses in the Septuagint, or Greek, version of the Exodus story.) This murmuring and controversy was an intrusion of the unclean into the community of the holy ones ("saints"; Philippians 1:1). The divisive behaviors were thus to be avoided from yet another angle, that of the sanctity of the community and of the One who dwelled in its midst.

Paul closed his exhortation to unity with the topic that he introduced near its beginning: the joy that it would bring the apostle for them to continue to live in a manner worthy of the gospel he brought to them. In Philippians 2:16-18, he reminded the Philippians that he might, in fact, be facing execution—largely on account of bringing people like the Philippian Christians to a saving knowledge of God (hence the imagery of being a libation poured out over their own faith offering in 2:17). The hearts of the believers were likely moved by this imagery and by the fact that they could make their partner's sacrifice a meaningful one by so simple an act as setting aside their internal differences.

RECOVERING A RIGHT FOCUS

• Paul twice urged the congregation to take thought for what mattered for their collective deliverance on the day of Christ (Philippians 1:9-11; 2:12-13) as a remedy for dissension in the church. What was at stake for them? How can murmuring and arguing be mistaken for dealing with an issue instead of "hand wringing" and avoiding it?

• In your experience, do most eruptions of discord center on matters of less than eternal significance? What would individual Christians need to be willing to do in order to "back down" in such situations, so that harmony could be restored?

• Rips, tears, and open wounds in bodies tended to render an animal or person "unclean" according to Leviticus. Why would pollution language therefore be a fitting image for dissension and strife in the church? Read 1 Corinthians 12. How does the metaphor of the church as Jesus' body and each believer as a body part promote cooperation and harmony?

• If concern for Paul's joy motivated the Philippians to seek harmony, concern for Jesus' joy should motivate us all the more. Read John 17:20-26 and discuss its implications for church life.

IN CLOSING

• The first half of Philippians raises some substantial issues concerning individual discipleship and living and working together in a community of believers. What issue or issues have been most challenging to you, and why? Where have you heard God's unmistakable word to you in this study?

• Recite aloud and reflect again upon the Christ hymn in Philippians 2:5-11. Pray for God's help in remaining mindful of Christ's mind in your interactions with others through the days and weeks ahead.

VI DISPUTE, DIVISION; HARMONY, UNITY

Two Model Servants
Read Philippians 2:19-30

Philippians 2:19-30 may appear at first to introduce a wholly new subject, marking the close of the discussion of the mind that leads to unity and harmony within the church. One might suspect that Paul had turned to the epistolary convention of the "letter of recommendation." He praised the worth of Epaphroditus (who was returning to his congregation in Philippi with this letter) and of Timothy (whom Paul also hoped to send to the congregation once the outcome of Paul's trial became known). Paul also requested that Epaphroditus and Timothy be received in a manner suited to their service and honor.

Paul has not left his primary topic, however, with the commendation of these two brothers. Each of them is set forward as a living example of what it looks like to have the mind of Christ. Timothy distinguished himself among the coterie of Christian missionaries because he was "genuinely concerned for your welfare" (Philippians 2:20). (The Greek suggests colorfully that "there is no one whose soul is equal to his.") Timothy thus stood in stark contrast with some unnamed others who were "seeking their own interests, not those of Jesus Christ" (2:21). This contrast intentionally recalled the exhortation in 2:4, offering Timothy as a person in whom the principle commended there could be seen in action.

The second example would be even more personal for the congregation, since Epaphroditus was one of their own number. Epaphroditus was an emissary on behalf of the Philippian Christians and brought Paul a gift from his friends in Philippi to assist him in his confinement (Philippians 4:10-20). On the journey, Epaphroditus fell ill and even came close to dying—all in the service of the congregation and of Paul. As a person who risked his life for "the work of Christ" (2:30), Epaphroditus, too, became a living example of one who put the interests of others ahead of his own interests, and, in a manner of speaking, was obedient almost to the point of death.

In this way, Paul bolstered his exhortation with a number of examples of commendable Christian behavior. Christ, of course, set the high water mark and the standard; but there were also models close at hand in the persons of Timothy and Epaphroditus. Paul engaged in a lengthy paragraph of self-disclosure so as to continue to provide useful models after which his friends in Philippi were to pattern themselves. People like Epaphroditus who embodied the mind of Christ were to be held in honor (Philippians 2:29), not those who insisted on receiving recognition or on having matters go their way. In the church, unlike the world, precedence and esteem cannot come because individuals have sought and fought for such recognition but only because they have, ironically, put others first out of a sincere love.

TWO MODEL SERVANTS

• What were Paul's purposes in these commendatory paragraphs concerning Timothy and Epaphroditus? How did Timothy reflect the kind of character Paul wanted to continue to nurture in the Philippian congregation, particularly in light of Philippians 2:1-11? What can you reconstruct of Epaphroditus' ministry on behalf of the congregation and Paul from 2:25-30 and 4:10-20? What challenges did Epaphroditus face in the execution of this ministry? What did Paul hold up as commendable in Epaphroditus? How might Paul's honoring of these two men have moved the hearers to respond?

• Are there people in your local church, in the local networks of your denomination, or otherwise within your sphere of acquaintance who embody the kind of qualities that Paul promoted in Philippians 2:1-11? How do these people reflect the rejection of conceit and selfish ambition and embody the other-centered service that makes the mind of Christ shine through them? How might you encourage them and also be shaped and refined by their example?

Beware of Dogs
Read Philippians 3:1–4:1

It is tempting to read Philippians 3:2 as a sign that the kind of Judaizing teachers who had upset the Galatian Christians had now made their way into the Philippian congregation, but this was not likely to have been the case. If these rival teachers were indeed a threat to the gospel in Philippi, Paul would have provided something of the sustained argumentation against the necessity of circumcision and other topics such as one finds in Galatians. Rather, Paul called to mind the Judaizing Christians to provide a negative example, a foil for Paul's own example that he immediately developed in 3:4-16. The call to "look out for the dogs" in 3:2 is matched by Paul's later instruction to "observe those who live according to the example" of Paul, which they themselves are explicitly called to imitate (3:17). Mention of these Judaizers may also continue to transfer the Philippians' sense of competition and enmity away from fellow believers inside the group toward people outside the group.

In this chapter, Paul continues to cultivate a picture of what it looks like to have the mind of Christ as one pursues the goal of the Christian life. This portrait of the mind of Christ is variously described as attaining the resurrection from the dead (Philippians 3:10-11), the "prize of the heavenly call" (3:14), and the heavenly city (3:20). The way to pursue this goal successfully is to be entirely Christ centered in one's focus and ambitions and to refuse to place one's confidence "in the flesh" (3:3). The Judaizers taught that physical circumcision had such value in God's sight that Gentile Christians needed to accept this sign upon their own bodies. To Paul, however, this meant placing one's confidence in a mark in the flesh rather than fully relying on Christ's faithfulness to those who trust and seek him.

When it came to ethnic and religious credentials, Paul had enjoyed every privilege in the estimation of his fellow Jews. His parents had passed on to him a perfect pedigree in the house of Israel, and he had distinguished himself by his zeal for living out Torah's prescriptions (Philippians 3:4-6). Nevertheless, he considered all these credentials by which he formerly built himself up and measured himself against other people as "rubbish" (translated more accurately and picturesquely as "garbage" or "dung"; 3:7-8). He felt this way because he had found that attaining Jesus and the life Jesus confers to be of immensely greater value than the precedence and esteem he had tried to forge for himself prior to encountering Jesus.

At this point, a parallel with Christ's example in Philippians 2:5-11 begins to emerge. Both Christ and Paul had serious claims to recognition and preeminence, but both "regarded" these claims as being of less value than journeying where God commanded and discovering the reward that God has prepared for those who go forth in obedience (2:6-7; 3:7-8). Following Jesus' example, Paul, too, emptied himself of the claims to precedence he could have made on account of his Israelite heritage and his achievements in that way of life. He modeled Jesus' willingness to disregard credentials and Jesus' refusal to accept the privileges that normally came with those credentials. Just as Jesus came to have his honor universally acclaimed only by following the path of renouncing those claims, so also the follower of Jesus can only hope to enjoy the honor God bestows by giving up the attempt to make a name for himself or herself, both in the world and in the church.

In Philippians 3:8b-11, Paul gives us a glimpse of the passion that drove his own discipleship and ministry. The only prize worth seeking and winning in this life, for him, was Christ himself. Paul sought intimate fellowship with Jesus, which entailed being willing to embrace not only the power of Christ's resurrected life flowing into and through one's own service but also "the sharing of his [Christ's] sufferings." Paul had his fill of sufferings (see 2 Corinthians 4:7-12; 6:3-10; 11:16-33), but it was precisely when he was drained of his own resources and self-reliance that he discovered the power and encouragement that came from God alone. It was this power, and not his own determination, that sustained Paul's faith in the face of crushing adversity and that empowered a ministry that changed the Roman Empire (see 2 Corinthians 4:7, 16-18). The Philippians themselves, through their endurance of outside, hostile opposition to their confession of Christ, were also invited to share in this power (Philippians 1:27-30).

The process for attaining Christ and the prize of a res-

urrected life in the city of God entails becoming conformed (*summorphizomenos*) into the likeness of Christ's
death (Philippians 3:10). This takes the reader directly
back to the Christ hymn of 2:5-11, where the "form" root
(*morph-*) was also prominently featured ("the form of
God" to "the form of a slave"; 2:6-7). Following Paul's
advice in 2:1-11 is not just a matter of church life; it is the
way to live in witness to one's hope for eternal life.
"Sharing in Christ's sufferings" means both enduring
hardship out of loyalty and obedience to Jesus and relin-
quishing the desire to be "first" in the community or to
have one's own interests and will served. In this kind of
"sharing," one takes the "form of a servant" to one's sisters and brothers, which is the only way also to be a servant of God.

BEWARE OF DOGS

• Given Paul's own testimony, how did Paul feel about himself as a Jew?
What kind of standing within the Jewish community do you think he
enjoyed? What happened to that standing when he became a follower
and preacher of the gospel? Philippians 3:7-11 might be read as Paul's
reflection on his own life choices and the losses he voluntarily chose out
of regard for the richness of knowing Jesus. What does his testimony
tell you about the value of following Jesus? How might his example
embolden you to relinquish any hold you keep on status in the eyes of
others so as to be free to follow Jesus more closely and completely?

• Being conformed to the likeness of Christ in his death—that is, to the
mind of Christ as celebrated in Philippians 2:5-11—can be understood
as the path to embodying the righteousness that comes from God.
Why would such righteousness be preferable to establishing oneself as
righteous based on following the prescriptions of a written code like
the Torah? Why would the latter be a hindrance to the former? Think
about Paul's own experience, where zeal for Torah led him to become
an enemy of the church.

> • What did the "sharing in Christ's sufferings" and "the power of his resurrection" signify for Paul? Reviewing the texts from Second Corinthians may help open up Paul's perspective here. How have you known this fellowship and this power in your own walk of discipleship?

Running for the Prize
Read Philippians 3:12-16

Paul wanted to provide his friends with a model for what Christian maturity looks like in action (Philippians 3:15). In so doing, he continued to describe what it means to refuse to place one's confidence "in the flesh" or otherwise to claim recognition or pride of place in others' eyes on the basis of one's achievements. To this end, he shared his own mindset as he moved forward in discipleship, using images highly suggestive of an athlete running a race. A runner focuses on the next steps of a race, straining ever forward toward the finish line, concentrating on the finish line and its prize. In such an enterprise, there is little room for looking back at how far one has traveled, taking pride in having made it halfway to the finish line, or boasting of being a better runner than one's fellow racers. All such thoughts would be dangerous distractions to the one who hoped to win the race. Rather, the person's whole being — mind, will, ambition, and strength — must be focused on what lies ahead.

Paul no longer speaks merely about leaving behind the pre-Christian credentials he leaned upon for recognition in a community and for a sense of his own self-worth (Philippians 3:4-6). He had already dealt with those in 3:7-8. When Paul wrote from that prison late in his life as a Christian missionary and said that he did not focus on "what lies behind" (3:13), he included also his astounding accomplishments in the service of Christ. Paul had occasion to observe in Corinth the dangers of holding on to those achievements. There, Christians used their spiritual knowledge, their spiritual gifts, their attachment to particular Christian teachers, and their service to the community as claims to enjoy privileged status in the community. The result was a church that was deeply divided along several different lines.

Paul likely perceived such a dynamic to be at work in the rift between Syntyche and Euodia, two prominent leaders of the community. Each one, reflecting on her service to the church in Philippi, her importance in the history of the growth of that congregation, and her sacrifices made on behalf of the church, no doubt felt she had an impressive claim on the right to have a say in where the church should go from there. Perhaps you yourself have heard — or thought — "After all I've done for this church, I can't believe anyone would oppose me on this!" In setting forward his own mind, Paul provided a potent remedy for this kind of competitive, self-focused, and ultimately divisive thinking.

There is simply no place in this race for stopping to take pride in one's achievements along the road, or, even more to the point, for insisting that the other runners run your way and to your rhythms on the basis of how much you have invested in running the race. Instead, all the focus is to be on Christ (Philippians 3:8-11) and on the goal of the race, which is not winning petty power struggles on earth but rather being invited into the commonwealth of God in heaven (Philippians 3:20).

We should not ignore the fact that Paul continued to acknowledge the work of Jesus in this race. It was Jesus who first took hold of Paul, and only on the basis of Jesus' laying hold on him could Paul hope to lay hold one day on the prize (Philippians 3:12). Twice before in this letter, the reader has encountered a similar sentiment (see 1:6, 11; 2:12-13). This is another prescription against getting puffed up and insisting on recognition in the church (or getting one's own way because of what one has done for the church). Ultimately, it is Jesus who is behind our every success, all our fruitful labor (see 1 Corinthians 4:7). What we have done must tend toward recognition of Jesus' faithfulness toward the church, not our own accomplishments.

RUNNING FOR THE PRIZE

• Perhaps you have watched or even participated in a one-mile race. Imagine yourself in the midst of such a race. Where is your focus? Why would you run better if your focus were directed forward, toward the goal of running in the first place, than if it were directed backward, toward the ground you already covered, or sideways, toward the other runners? What did Paul hope to convey by applying this image to the Christian life? Why would "resting on one's laurels" pose a hazard to the Christian runner?

• Paul's particular concern was the unity and harmony of the Christian group. Why would remembering all one's accomplishments for Christ and for the church and calling attention to those contributions to the life of the church feed one's own spirit of rivalry? Why would this attitude motivate someone to want his or her own way in the church and to demand recognition? How would this posture also deny one's own dependence on Christ? How, then, would taking on Paul's own mindset as expressed in Philippians 3:12-16 contribute to the health of the church?

• It is possible that the Spirit is using Paul's words to call you to repent of some particular controversy in which you have played a part or to confess that your focus has been too much on what you have done and too little on what Christ has done and what lies ahead for you to do in concert with the whole church. If so, use this opportunity to repent and to receive redirection and refreshment from God.

Living as Friends of the Cross
Read Philippians 3:17–4:1

The pattern of clarifying the godly mind by considering it alongside its contrast in the earthly mind continues in Philippians 3:17–4:1. Paul invited the believers to imitate him and to observe those who followed the example he had given them (3:17). Then he immediately called to mind another way of walking that is completely contradictory to the way of Christ (3:18-19). Paul rounded out the paragraph by recalling the hope that set the Philippian believers apart from the way of life that is focused merely on earthly ambitions or desires (3:20-21). He reminded them of the ultimate motivation for distancing their own conduct from the conduct of the "enemies of the cross of Christ" (3:18).

Paul spoke about these "enemies of the cross" with tears, probably because he had in mind those who considered themselves to be Christians but had lost their focus on the heavenly prize and had fallen back into the pursuit of earthly enjoyments. Paul had often encountered such people in his career — from the Judaizing missionaries in Galatia, to the rival apostles in Corinth, to the members of his team who deserted him (2 Timothy 4:9-10), to worldly minded Christians whose hearts remained fixed on the indulgence of the flesh and the fleshly mind.

The way Paul described them in Philippians 3:19 suggests that they served the interests of their own person, whether a desire of the body, a craving for worldly honor gained in a worldly way, or any other temporal object of their heart. Such people walked in the error of Esau, who relinquished an eternal heritage for the sake of a short-lived pleasure (see Hebrews 12:15-17). They were "enemies of the cross" because they resisted the work of the cross in their own lives, refusing to take on the mind of Jesus therein revealed.

Paul's friends in Philippi were not to behave as such shallow believers. As they conformed themselves to the mind of Christ, they confirmed their commitment to Jesus' promise that he would return to transform their mortal bodies into his immortal likeness (Philippians 3:21). They were encouraged not to turn aside from this great hope for the sake of satisfying any desire that belonged to the "body of humiliation" (3:21), whether the desire to come out first in an argument, the desire to get one's own way, or the desire for recognition. Rather, each one was to live as a friend of the cross of Jesus, honoring the way of life and the mindset that Jesus revealed by imitating them in the here and now.

LIVING AS FRIENDS OF THE CROSS

• Reflect on the description of the "enemies of the cross" in Philippians 3:18-19. What does it mean to "worship one's belly"? to take pride in what is actually disgraceful? to set one's mind on earthly things? Return to 2:1-11, where Paul described motives and attitudes that are "friendly" toward the cross and hostile toward the way of life Christ himself lived. To what extent have you, as a believer, lived as an enemy of the cross? In what ways does Paul's letter challenge you to live more as a friend to the cross?

• Philippians 3:20-21 (see also 3:10-11) reintroduces topics of eschatology into a discussion of how to live the Christian life. Why was it important for Paul to keep holding up this goal, this prize, before the hearers? How did it help them raise their ambitions again from "earthly things"?

Common Ground
Read Philippians 4:2-9

The way has been paved for Paul to request specifically that Syntyche and Euodia lay aside their differences or desist from their divisive struggle and "be of the same mind in the Lord" (Philippians 4:2). This request recalled specifically the language of 2:2, where Paul called for the whole congregation to "be of the same mind." No doubt, these women would have reflected on their particular quarrel as they heard Paul's exhortations to unity and harmony, seeking one another's interests, and laying aside conceit and rivalry. We might balk at the idea that Paul wrote Philippians 1:27–4:1 largely to bring about the reconciliation of these two women. Those who have seen what can happen when two leading congregational figures disagree and turn the issue into a personal one of ego, wounded pride, and hurt feelings over a perceived lack of proper appreciation for their contributions realize that such a situation begs for a timely intervention, however.

We should pay particular attention to Philippians 4:3. First, Paul addressed some "loyal companion" among the readership. Scholars have tried to determine who this person might have been, neglecting the possibility that Paul intended every person in that congregation to consider himself or herself a "true yoke-fellow" (as it is translated in the KJV and RSV) of the apostle and thus be entrusted with steering Syntyche and Euodia toward reconciliation. The responsibility of believers is not to take sides in a conflict between two of their fellow Christians but to guide them toward reconciliation and harmony. Second, in speaking of each woman as someone who had struggled alongside Paul for the sake of the gospel and as someone whose name was inscribed in the book of life, Paul reminded Euodia of Syntyche's worth and Syntyche of Euodia's worth. Neither one of them should have been competing against the other or involved in a dispute seeking to win at the expense of the other. They were partners in the advancement of the gospel and partners in eternity, and they needed to regard each other in that light.

Philippians 4:4-9 contains some of the more familiar verses from this letter. In this section, Paul directed the focus of the congregation back toward their common ground. The first injunction, to "rejoice in the Lord" (4:4; see also 3:1), is a potent remedy for any divisive spirit. Rejoicing in the Lord means taking delight in what God has done for the believer, in life as God's gift, and in the work of God through other members of the congregation and throughout the church universal. Rejoicing in the Lord is wholly centered on God, on the excellence of God's character, and on the perfection of God's gifts and so cannot co-exist in the heart with selfish ambition or conceit, with rivalry or division.

Paul reminded the congregation of the astounding resource they had in God—a God who was near to them and who stood ready to break into this age and usher in the Kingdom. Paul encouraged his friends to frequent God's presence in prayer, laying before God the concerns of their hearts, so that they could move from anxiety to the "peace of God" that defies human understanding. He encouraged them to infuse their prayer with gratitude for God's past provisions in time of need and for God's good and wise attention and answer to their new concerns. Finally, Paul called the hearers to focus their minds on what is good. It is so easy to fixate on what is wrong or to allow the mind to be polluted with what is worldly or base. By training the mind to ponder what is honorable and pleasing in God's sight, one is more likely to do these very things and to move others to do so. And, indeed, "doing" is the final word of this series of exhortations. The instruction Paul gave in life and in speech is to be acted out in the daily lives of the believers (Philippians 4:9).

COMMON GROUND

• Unity and rivalry have been major topics throughout the letter. Review Philippians 1:15-18, 27; 2:1-11; 3:12-16. How would Syntyche and Euodia have heard those earlier parts of the letter? We know nothing of the particulars of their disagreement, only that it was important to Paul that they return to harmony and cooperation for the sake of the whole group. What would it take for the two women to come to terms? How has Paul prepared them to pay the personal and public costs of seeking reconciliation? It is easy for two people, when they disagree, to form a correspondingly negative picture of each other. How does Paul's disclosure of his estimation of each of them in 4:2-3 help restore their image of each other?

• What does it mean to "rejoice in the Lord"? What has been your experience of the genuine joy that comes from the Lord? If you do not experience that joy now, what has taken your focus off the Lord; or what stands between you and joy? What journey would you need to take to get back to (or to move forward to) joy in the Lord?

• Reflect on your experience of prayer and privately write out a response. Have you felt free to lay all your concerns before God? To what extent has prayer allowed you to defeat anxiety? What has to happen in prayer for you to move from anxiety to peace?

• At this point, it might be helpful to synthesize what you have learned about Paul's vision for harmony and unity in the church. Why is this important? What attitudes toward one another and toward one's own purpose should an individual adopt so as to contribute to this spirit of harmony? What strategies might need to be employed to help two persons at odds in the church achieve reconciliation with each other in the Lord?

Paul's "Thank You" Note
Read Philippians 4:10-23

Paul closed (and opened) his letter to the Philippians with the theme of partnership (see 1:3-7). There, Paul thanked God for their partnership; here, Paul thanked the

Philippians directly for the most recent symbol of their partnership, namely, the unspecified gift (most likely money) that the congregation had sent through Epaphroditus. We are reminded again here of the special, even unique, relationship Paul enjoyed with this church among the many he had founded (4:15-16). The Philippians were his partners at the beginning of his missionary work in Macedonia and Achaia; they continued to be his partners in his confinement late in his life.

Two aspects of this "Thank You" note require special notice. First, Paul basically said that although he appreciated the gift and the love that stood behind it (Philippians 4:10-14), he really did not need the money. We should not read this as though Paul belittled the gift, however. On the one hand, he wanted to affirm to his friends that they and their concerns were more important to him than the funds (4:10, 17). On the other hand, he was simply still sharing his mind and heart with his friends. Indeed, Paul had advanced to such a deep dependence on Jesus that neither want nor abundance threatened to subvert his loyalty to God or to derail the focus of his service.

Second, although Paul was the direct recipient of the gift, the Philippians' act of sharing with Paul was also, mysteriously, a gift to God. It was a liturgical act, a sacrifice that had value in God's sight and that God had accepted (Philippians 4:18). Paul expressed confidence that God would also respond generously to the Philippians, in a strange twist of the normal flow of reciprocity. Paul himself should return some gift to the Philippians, but he was in no position to think about such a return at the time. God is in no way indebted by a gift, being the Giver and Source of all. Nevertheless, God looks with favor on the generous act of God's children and will remember their own character when they call upon God for help in time of need (4:19). Thus, in God's economy, no generous act goes without reward.

PAUL'S "THANK YOU" NOTE

• How might having plenty of food, clothing, and the other necessities of life (not to mention all the extras) pose a threat to remaining focused on Christ, on the prize of resurrection, and on the service to which God calls us? Why, from the other side, might having too little of these things pose a threat as well? Paul had matured to the point where neither penury nor abundance could master him. What was the "secret" that he had learned? How does Philippians 4:13, which is all too often quoted out of context, shed light on this "secret"?

• Some of us are put off by the preacher who says, "Give your money to support my ministry, and God will bless you financially," and so forth. How did Paul distinguish himself from the religious or philosophical huckster that was also common in his day?

• The view of God's provision articulated in Philippians 4:19 seems to be given fuller expression in 2 Corinthians 9:6-14. How does Paul's theology of money—that resources are provided by God to enable generosity and also that God favors those who are themselves gracious—line up with your own thinking about making money and about stewardship?

IN CLOSING

• Review the insights, challenges, or instructions that you have encountered in the study of Philippians that you have heard as God's word for you. What is God calling you to do in response to your study in the next stage of your life of discipleship?

• Pray for the unity and harmony of your local congregation. Pray for humility and love to replace rivalry and divisive dissent throughout your whole denomination and, indeed, the church universal. Pray for the mind of Christ to take even deeper root in your own mind so that you may serve the goal of a harmonious and united church.